HOW TO PROFIT FROM THE COMING SHARE BOOM

Michael Walters

SCOPE
INTERNATIONAL
LIMITED

Published by
Scope International Ltd.,
62 Murray Road,
Waterlooville,
Hants PO8 9JL
Great Britain

1st Edition 1992
By Michael Walters

For questions and further information contact the author by mail or by fax in care of the publisher.

British Library Cataloguing in-Publication Data.
A catalogue record for this book is available from the British Library.

ISBN 0 906619 37 8

Phototypeset by Barbara James Typesetting, Rowlands Castle, Hampshire
Printed by Hartnolls, Bodmin, Cornwall

CONTENTS

INTRODUCTION

You can make money on the stock market. It need not be complicated. Anyone with simple common sense and a little cash to spare can do it. This book is devoted to helping you, guiding you through the tricks and the traps in simple, straightforward language. It can be done. Hundreds of thousands of private investors did it in the great share boom of the eighties. Hundreds of thousands more will do it in the boom which is coming in the nineties.

This time, hopefully, anyone who has read this book will know when to take their profits, to avoid the crash which caught so many in October 1987. There were hard lessons to be learnt then – but for those prepared to listen and learn, the benefits will be reaped in the years to come.

Be under no illusion. Despite Tory Government talk about encouraging individual share ownership, life has become more difficult, more expensive, altogether less comfortable for the private investor over the past five years.

Consistently I have fought for the small investor in the City pages of the *Daily Mail,* to little avail when it comes to getting officialdom to change things. But I have helped run several dubious share pushing firms out of business, recovering tidy sums for many investors, and have killed some particularly greedy share schemes.

All of this has helped convince me of the need for a guide which places great emphasis on dodging the pitfalls of private investment, and which attends more to the practical realities of what happens when you try to trade shares than to the arid, misleading theory.

Yet none of it has put me off share investment for the individual, so long as you have your eyes open. Never mind what they tell you, the stock market is manipulated. It does dance to the tune played by the big money. After Big Bang in October 1986 changed the rules, the big boys have got more powerful, the small players much weaker.

In the old days, with brokers and jobbers dealing face to face, and men scuttling round the trading floor, there were abuses. But they were on on a more human scale. You could not rook a man too savagely when you knew you would meet him every working day. Now the trade is international, conducted by young dealers who may never meet, on computer screens. The touch of a button can wipe millions off share values, or put them on.

Billions of pounds have been invested in high-tech offices and machinery. Hundreds of milions have been lost. Some of the mightiest banking and investment names in the world have gone bust, or retired hurt. Those who remain are competing desperately to make money from a more complex, nastier world. They spend much of their time snatching quick profits from each other as momentary opportunities flash across the screens, a kind of real-life corporate Pacman computer game.

They cannot manipulate the economy. But they can swing the market, or large chunks of it, from day to day at certain times. Officially, they say such things cannot happen. But they do. Ruthlessly. When a big investment house has, say, £100m of shares to sell, it can use the computer systems to cast a smoke screen, mislead the competition, and manipulate the market briefly one way or another. Frequently, some houses use their computing power and cash resources to play with the futures markets and the real stock market to create profitable opportunites.

Never mind. They need the money, poor dears. Often their jobs are on the line. Few outsiders really understand it. Small investors have no chance.

Do not let it deter you. When the economic situation allows, the big money will be devoted to manipulating prices upwards as far and as fast as they can. The big players need a strong stock market. As they push it higher, you can benefit, clinging to their coat-tails. Their international games will help change the whole mood, pumping new life into the market for smaller company shares where so many individual investors love to play – and where the big boys are slow to catch on.

Keep your wits about you, and you have nothing to fear. You really can make money on the stock market. All you have to do is to buy when prices are low, and sell when they are high.

It sounds elementary, of course. So obvious that it hardly bears saying. Pause for a moment, and think about it. Why is it that we all know it is true, and yet so few investors – large or small – succeed in doing it?

Perhaps it is the thrill of the game. It is so easy to get sucked into the day-to-day excitement and to lose sight of the main objective. Everyone gets busy watching prices, analysing profit moves, trying to read the chairman's mind, hanging on for that extra penny or two, and they forget to step back and see where it is all going. Before they know it, the economy is running into trouble, the market is overheated, and shares are on the slide.

Suddenly, yesterday's fat paper profit is today's real loss. What a pity we got so greedy. Better hang on, and hope it all comes back? Will it ever come back? Of course. Or some of it will.

The nightmare still sits on many an investors' shoulder. It happened in October, 1987 – a classic share slump. No-one playing the market then will forget it, especially if they lived in the South of England. It was uncanny. While prices went into free fall, a hurricane howled across the land, bringing trees tumbling down, tearing tiles off roofs, and sending chimneys crashing through ceilings. The *Financial Times* Index lost 500 points in two trading sessions. It had never before lost more than 70 points in a single day. Shares galore shed a quarter of their value before many investors realised what was happening. Small company shares became almost impossible to sell.

It was the end of the share world as many small investors knew it. Some retired, licking their wounds, hoping to play another day. Others were so badly burnt that they will never be back. A few – the quicker or the more cautious – blessed their foresight in selling ahead of the slump.

The Crash of October 1987 looks easy to understand, with hindsight. It had all got too much, the price of many shares had gone beyond reasonable bounds, millions of small investors were coming in to gamble for the first time, and the great push onwards and upwards simply could not be sustained. The market hit the kind of buying frenzy which tends to occur near the top of all great booms. As usual, the boom gave way to a slump.

How easy it is to write such a glib, predictable line. If only we had all been so smart at the time. Yet it is remarkable just how predictable it should have been to anyone who did step back and look, anyone who gave a thought to what has happened in the past. The lesson is clear, time and again. As sure as night follows day, stock market slump follows stock market boom. Then it rolls around – the slump in turn is followed by a boom.

That is the reason for this book. Nothing clever – no secret formula guaranteed to make a fortune. Simply the basic application of a little common sense, plus a collection of old lessons which are worth learning anew after the experience of the eighties. And a determination to tell it like it is in the market, not they way they pretend it works.

The old lessons do work, believe me. As a financial journalist for thirty years, and an investor for much of that time, I have been through the slump of the mid-seventies, and the Great

Crash of 1987. I lost money in both. Each time, I started with little capital, and made a respectable sum before it all went wrong – not a fortune, but enough for most people to envy. First time around, I lost it all. Second time, starting from practically nothing, I made about the same amount, though it was worth less because of inflation. Second time, I spent a fair bit while I had it, kept some, and lost about half. I like to think I had learnt something by experience.

Third time – and there will be another boom and a third chance for me – I plan to do better. What I make, I will keep – or most of it anyway. Talking to other investors, tipsters, and men who have built substantial businesses, they have similar experiences. We all made silly mistakes. We look back with amazement at how daft we were. And hope to learn from it.

None of us has come up with anything too profound. We laugh in disbelief at our stupidity. There are no great insights which will make us a fortune in the future. No matter how big the businesses most of these people have built, how much they have made and lost, it all so often comes back to common sense, and basic principles. The secret is to keep your head, stick to what you know, and what ought to be right.

This book hammers away at the common sense lessons, and reinforces them with others learnt the hard way. It is written from experience, not from cold theory. I know what it means, how it feels, to make money and lose it on the stock market. Winning is marvellous for a while, lifts your whole day, and then you become blase and cocky. Losing hits you in the pit of the stomach – then passes. There is always (unless you have been really daft) another chance.

The boom is coming. It always does. And when the market is booming, most shares go up. Then people start saying slightly scornfully; 'Any fool could make money in this market.' It is not true. Only the arrogant and ignorant say such things. Making real money in shares is never that easy. But in a rising market, the odds do swing significantly your way. It IS easier, the risks ARE more modest. The chance of a costly failure is much smaller.

Whatever anyone tries to tell you, playing the stock market is a form of gambling. If you object to that, do not do it. Do not buy this book. But when you bet on the stock market, the bet can stay alive for much longer than anything in a betting shop. And you have ample opportunity to retrieve some of your stake money if things are not going your way.

Unless you are playing more sophisticated games, you only lose all of your money in shares when the company you choose goes bust. There has been a spate of company collapses in recent years. But few public companies go bust in a rising market, when the economy is improving. Anyone who reads this book should be able to tell when trouble is looming, and sell long before the end. Common sense is crucial. Playing the stock market is not difficult. Anyone can do it. All you need is a little money – the kind you can afford to lose – and a level head. As any of the millions who have made profits from the spate of privatisations over the past decade will know, buying and selling shares can be simple if you want it to be.

If you are sensible, there is nothing to fear. A careful investor, observing simple, basic rules, can do as well as any of the massive City houses, perhaps better.

The sophisticates have no monopoly of stock market skills – nor do they lack their portion of stock market stupidity. How well I recall the so-called top analyst at big-name house who insisted that Brent Walker shares had assets of £10, and were worth at least half that. The same firm repeatedly backed Maxwell Communication Corporation as I cast doubt on it through the years. And a chap with a most impressive title tried to calm my fears about a controversial retailer – his company was advising it, of course – without even being aware of a major item raising eyebrows in the published accounts.

When any share soars, the number of small investors enjoying the ride will always be greater than the number of big City institutions. But the City names will have more money involved. When a company goes bust and the receivers move in, there will usually be lashings of big City money locked in alongside the hundreds of small investors who will be taking a comparatively small hit. You know the cliche. The bigger they come, the harder they fall.

The private investor can move in and out much more easily than any City giant. The big boys get caught because when things go wrong, they have too many shares to sell, and no-one to buy them. The small investor may have to take a loss, but the chances of actually being able to sell at a reasonable price are much greater when you have only small quantities to sell.

Share investment can be enormously complicated, laden with computer-driven gobbledeygook. Or it can be as simple as backing a name you like, and watching what happens. You do not need to be clever. No-one can beat a lucky investor. Share portfolios picked with a pin do sometimes beat those compiled by the experts.

But it does pay to learn a little about the basics. You can swing the odds in your favour. There are simple traps to avoid, certain elementary ideas for spotting possible winners. The more you learn, the more you improve your chances. And the more you learn, the more fun you will have. It is a game, and it can be enormously rewarding, not just in cash terms. The elation of spotting a winner and seeing it come right can yield enormous satisfaction, even if the cash profit is modest.

Investment can be fun, and it should be. Get it right, and it can transform your life. You really can make enough profit to make a difference to the way you live. Some shares do leap ten-fold, a few rise 100-fold. If you have just £1,000 in one of them, it can change your life. You do not even need to pick a run-away winner. Just double your money once, then pick another share which doubles. Do it a third time, and your £1,000 is £8,000.

When the market is booming, lots of shares double, and do it in six months or a year. Lots of people pick them, and make worthwhile profits. They hit a few losers along the way, of course, but you would be astonished how many ordinary people quietly score tidy winnings on the stock market – when times are good. The biggest problem is resisting the temptation to keep playing when the game is over. You must know when to sell, to turn paper profits into hard cash.

Keeping the winnings is crucial. Too few investors actually take the profits they make. Paper profits are no good. The only ones which count are those in your bank account. Learning how and when to take profits is not difficult. The stop loss system I have advocated for twenty years is a simple, almost foolproof way of doing it. This book explains, at length, how it works. The real problem is mustering the self-discipline to do it. Bitter experience from the Crash of '87 has hammered the discipline home to me. Perhaps this book will help you to learn.

Be sure. The boom is coming. It may not be this year, or next. But it will come. It may not yield the phenomenal quick profits we saw in the mid-eighties, when many shares trebled or quadrupled in a year, and doubling your money in twelve months was almost commonplace. But it will offer the opportunity of substantial profits. Buying into a rising market can yield rewards which make other forms of investment look leaden-footed. Shares in hundreds of companies tumbled to a quarter, even a tenth of their peak price in the late eighties. Several went bust. Some of the survivors may never regain their peak, but some will – and many others will double or more along the way, while a whole new galaxy of stars will be discovered.

Make no mistake. There will be a stock market boom in the nineties. Quietly, several shares doubled or trebled in 1990, and in 1991. The whole market rose almost a quarter in 1991, and there was no shortage of shares which gained 50pc or more – in a year when we were bumping along the bottom of recession.

Towards the end of 1991 and as 1992 got under way, the alert investor could have spotted a rash of new players quietly taking their places, making ready for when the game really begins to hum again. In February, 1992, I tipped one tiny shell company at 4p on one Monday morning. Three days later, it was 7p, suspended while a new venture was pumped in. Of course I was lucky with my timing. Of course that was an exception. But some *Daily Mail* readers did buy it. They know the opportunities are opening up again.

Big money is there to be made, and some are already making it. It may not be easy to spot exactly where we are in the cycle, exactly when the boom is coming – but as we move on into the nineties, the boom is ahead, not behind us. The instant the economic scene allows it, the big money will come pouring back, generating profits for all. Who knows? The result of the General Election may have cleared the way.

This book is designed to help you cash in on the opportunity of the decade.

Good luck.

Michael Walters

CHAPTER ONE
THE BOOM IS COMING

Buy cheap, sell dear. That is the way to make money. Keep that in mind, and you will not go far wrong. It sounds so simple as to be almost silly. Of course that is what you do. But if it is so obvious, why is it that everyone does not do it? We all ought to be able to make a fortune.

That simple notion of buying cheap and selling dear is at the heart of this book. The whole idea is to try to help make it clear just what is cheap on the stock market, and what is dear.

The best place to start is with the big picture – the economy. That is why I am writing this book at this time. Nothing clever. Broadly speaking, shares are cheapest when everyone feels gloomiest. We all tend to feel gloomier when the economy is depressed. As it picks up, and more money starts to circulate, confidence rises, people begin to spend, and profits rise. We all feel better. Share prices rise, too. In practice, they see the boom coming, and begin to rise well before it actually gets here.

It is very easy to get confused about the economy. So many economists with so many opinions, so many solutions, so many mistakes. You know the jokes – lock twenty economists in a room, and you will get fifty opinions. Or the Yeltsin variation? Boris Yeltsin says one of his plans to take Russia forward means firing 750,000 soldiers from the Soviet army, and replacing them with 47 economists. Why? asks one of his comrades. Everyone knows that economists are so highly paid that it will cost just as much to keep 47 economists as 750,000 soldiers. 'Ah' says Yeltsin, 'just think how much more damage 47 economists can do.'

Economics can be frightening. But forget the jargon. As a prospective investor, all you really need to know is whether the economy is getting better, or getting worse. You do not need to be too smart to work that out. Your own instincts will tell you, and the headlines will make it clear. Rising interest rates, higher unemployment, falling profits – they all add up to a weaker economy. And vice versa.

The simple rule is to buy when the economy is down, and sell when it is roaring ahead. Nothing lasts forever. Sure as can be, good times will be followed by bad. No matter how grim it seems at the bottom, there will be better times.

If you can be smart enough to cling on to your cash at the top, when everything seems to be too good to be true, you will have it ready to invest when all seems too bad to bear, just right to reap the rewards of a return to prosperity. No matter what, cash is always worth much more in bad times than good.

Through history, good and bad times follow each other with unerring predictability. Whatever we might like to think, we never succeed in ordering our affairs well enough to achieve perfectly balanced prosperity. There is always something to throw us off. It is not just in economic affairs. Stock market commentators like Bob Beckman track all manner of cycles in nature. Beckman's books like *The Downwave* and *Into the Upwave* have examples galore. Bill Houston also deals graphically with such things in *How Your Business Can Profit From The Recession*, another Scope International publication. Even natural forces, like the eruption of the mighty Mount Pinatubo volcano in the Phillipines, can impact on world economies and the stock market.

You do not have to agree with the interpretation Beckman and Houston put on everything to admire the study they have devoted to cycles, and to appreciate that we are locked into cycles galore. In stock market terms, every schoolboy knows about the South Sea Bubble of 1720. That was not the first speculative boom and slump. Nor the last. More recently, we have had the Great Crash of 1929, the Secondary Banking Collapse of 1974, and another Great Crash in October 1987 – followed by booms, every one of them. And in between, there has been a series of lesser rises and falls.

All of the more recent crashes were linked to periods of economic decline. Effectively, the stock market anticipated economic troubles. For those who were ready to step back, it was possible to see that the economy was getting overheated in the twenties, seventies, and eighties, and was due for a setback. Anyone who managed to do that, and was wary of the market as a result, did very well.

It is not the purpose of this book to try to convert everyone into an economic genius. It is not necessary. You can do very well in the stock market without it. Go back to our basic assumption – the economy is labouring, near the bottom of a recession. As it recovers, so shares will move higher. While it is depressed, the odds have been tilted in favour of the new investor. When the market reflects the economic recovery, share prices will be still higher. So long as you sell before it starts falling away again – and there is a crucial chunk of the book explaining when to sell – your chances of doing well have been vastly increased.

It is as well, though, to outline some of the economic fundamentals, the kind of things which indicate most clearly how the economy is moving.

INTEREST RATES

In the nineties, interest rates are the main lever the Government has left itself to influence the economy. Interest rates govern the price of money, the most basic commodity used by industry. On their own, they can provide a crude but effective guide to whether or not it is time to invest. When interest rates are high, put your cash into whatever yields the highest return for the longest fixed period. Keep clear of investments which do not give a fixed return – like Ordinary shares in companies. As interest rates fall, shift out of fixed return investments (whose capital values will be rising), and into those which give a return which will rise in line with profits – like shares.

A SIMPLE RULE

At its crudest, it is almost possible to advance an iron law of profits for the patient investor. If you can shut your eyes to all else, you will do well by putting your cash into fixed interest securities, like Government securities, when interest rates are 15pc or above. Sit with them until interest rates fall – as they will eventually – and when rates drop below 10pc, switch into shares. That is a crude, over-simplified system which requires the minimum of action. The turning points may only occur at five-yearly intervals, perhaps more quickly, perhaps more slowly. There will be false dawns and temptations along the way. You will almost certainly switch too early, and miss the very best returns. Yet if you have the patience to follow the system, you will outperform the average investor – though it does require a great deal of patience, and self-restraint almost to the point of paralysis.

High interest rates clog everything up, make business difficult all round. They raise the cost of borrowing, and make it more expensive to buy plant and machinery, and to provide the capital to buy the raw materials and pay the labour needed to meet the orders which will eventually yield profit. Superficially attractive to investors on fixed returns, they actually hurt them, too, since they almost always occur in periods of high inflation.

High interest rates also raise the cost of long-term credit, like mortgages, and short term credit, like bank overdrafts and credit cards. That leaves people with less to spend, so orders fall, industry suffers, and the whole economy slows down. The number of jobs declines, so there are fewer people with money to spend, and so on. The whole downward spiral gathers pace, and we all end up poorer because of high interest rates.

REAL INTEREST

While the Government often choses to ignore it, concentrating for political advantage on the simple headline rate of interest, there is a crucial difference between nominal interest rates and real interest rates. Between October 1990, when we entered the European Monetary System with a cut in bank base rates from 15pc to 14pc, and October 1991, nominal interest rates came down 3½ points to 10½pc.

Over that same period, in fact, real interest rates soared from 3.1pc to 6.8pc. The real cost of borrowing had more than doubled.

How come? In the real world, it is impossible to ignore the cost of inflation. Nominal interest rates do not tell the true story. If you can borrow at 5pc a year (though we never bother with the fine print, quoted interest rates almost always cover the cost of money for a year) when the rate of inflation is 5pc, you are effectively paying nothing for the use of the money you have borrowed for a year.

In order to find the REAL cost of cash, you must deduct the rate of inflation from the nominal rate of interest. So if nominal interest rates were 14pc in October 1990, when inflation was a socking 10.9pc, the real rate of interest was a mere 3.1pc – not so bad. A year later, while nominal interest rates were down to 10.5pc, inflation had tumbled to 3.7pc. So the real cost of cash was 6.8pc – historically very expensive.

No wonder industry was still screaming with pain in the winter of 1991/1992, no matter how longingly the Government hailed the end of the recession. The true cost of borrowing was crippling. It might have looked as if falling interest rates guaranteed a stock market recovery on the back of an industrial boom. But anyone who counted the true cost of money could see that it was not so simple. Perhaps the worst of the pain was not over.

INFLATION

The rate of inflation is clearly closely linked to interest rates as another key economic indicator. Inflation is public enemy number one for most politicians, especially the Tories. In 1960s, investors were quite happy to see it jog along at 2pc or 3pc. It meant that profits appeared to move ahead nicely on paper. Come the seventies, and inflation over 25pc, and everyone was horrified. It had to be driven out of the system. In the nineties, the Tories declared war on it. Panic measures in the wake of the October 1987 Crash, however, pumped more money into the system, and sent inflation soaring. The fight against inflation helped deepen the recession of the early nineties as the Government cut back the supply of money and pushed interest rates up. At base, inflation arises from too much money chasing too few goods. Prices are pushed higher as people become ready to pay more to get what is available. Less money in circulation chokes inflation, and more expensive money makes for less money.

The impact of inflation on the economy is broadly similar to high interest rates – it pushes up the real cost of money, and the real cost of assets. While nominal profits are higher, they are worth less because money buys less and less. Crucially, inflation can be a killer for older investors on fixed incomes. It erodes the real worth of their income.

For investors, though the high profits which are reported in times of rapid inflation may appear good, it is an illusion. Profits are more valuable when inflation is lower, and the big investor will be more confident about buying shares when inflation is under control. No-one, though, wants to be caught in fixed interest investments when inflation is rising. Their capital value is eaten away. So when inflation is rising, the best defence is to be invested in shares of a company whose profits and asset value are advancing with inflation. That is the ultimate protection. The trick is to get out before inflation gets so high that it damages the economy, and plunges everything into recession.

In crude terms, you want to buy shares when inflation is low, and sit with them as it begins to rise. You should be looking to sell, to switch your profits into fixed interest investments as inflation peaks, and starts to fall.

EXCHANGE RATES

Interest rates and inflation are crucially caught up with what happens to the pound and other foreign exchange rates. After a long spell when the pound was, in theory, left to float free and find its own level, we entered the European Monetary System in the autumn of 1990. Everything got more complicated.

In fact, under Chancellor Nigel Lawson we had followed a plan of trying to link the value of sterling to the German mark for several years. The Treasury was quietly tracking the mark. When we entered the European Monetary System, we subscribed to the Exchange Rate Mechanism. That links the exchange rates of all of the EMS members.

All currencies are supposed to be confined to movements within either broad or narrow bands against each other. When a currency looks like breaking out, the EMS central banks are committed to moving in to the foreign exchange markets to buy or sell currencies to try to defend the rate. Ultimately, though, EMS members are expected to follow broad economic policies which ensure that their currencies conform. That is why the French had to raise interest rates in November 1991, though it did not suit their domestic economic needs.

The pound went in with a pledge to stay within a broad band, 3pc either side of a central rate of DM2.95 against the German mark. The German currency was the strongest in the system, and German aversion to inflation after the horrific experiences of the 1920s had encouraged the Bundesbank in following economic policies which had proved remarkably effective in securing a low inflation economy.

The idea was that if we linked our currency with the mark, we would be forced to follow policies which eventually brought our performance close to German levels – the convergence idea. In the first year, however, this was thrown off course by German unification. That brought a vast influx of demand from East Germany, and began to push up German inflation. That prompted the Germans to adopt a tough anti-inflation policy, with relatively high interest rates at a time when the United Kingdom and many others in Europe really needed lower interest rates to combat recession.

Thanks to membership of the Exchange Rate Mechanism, the UK could not cut interest rates to boost the domestic economy because it would have provoked a sterling crisis.

International investors would have switched from the low-yielding and insecure pound to the strong mark, which was bolstered by more attractive German interest rates.

DEVALUATION

Set all this against the background of a move to greater European political and monetary union, and you have the formula for considerable problems. In earlier times, the answer would have been to devalue the pound, either by a formal declaration that sterling would be exchangeable into other currencies at lower rates, or simply by letting it fall on the foreign exchange markets. This option was not easily available under ERM membership.

To re-align currency rates (the fancy new name for devaluation in our case) would have meant undermining the position of sterling in the European Monetary System. The rationale of the EMS is to move to relatively fixed exchange rates, and eliminate the uncertainties imposed on business by rates which are constantly shifting.

Devaluing the pound would help the economy by effectively reducing the price of exports from Britain, making our goods cheaper around the world. That, in theory, should pump extra demand into industry. At the same time, a cheaper pound means it costs us more to import. That should reduce the attractions of buying goods from abroad, and divert extra home demand into UK goods. The value of this is debatable, though in practice, devaluations have generally worked in the past, after a while.

MONEY SUPPLY

ERM membership has left the Government with interest rates as the main weapon to determine the direction of the economy and the fight against inflation. There is, however, the opportunity to tinker by altering tax rates, public spending, and the supply of money. An increased supply of money is frowned upon as inflationary, but the Autumn Statement in 1991 showed the Government weakening in its resolve with the approach of an election. Additional Government spending was committed to politically sensitive projects, health, education and transport. This in turn required a rise in the future Government borrowing, and acted as a way of pumping more money into the flat economy without cutting interest rates.

Amid all of this we have worries about rising unemployment versus soaring wage costs, whether our balance of payments (the level of imports compared with exports) will slump, how the price of oil will influence us (inflationary if it goes up, but helpful in some ways because we are a significant oil producer), and so on.

The complications are countless, and the various interpretations of them infinite. Tens of thousands of people make a very good living writing and debating them.

READING THE TREND

In the end, no-one knows the real answers. No-one gets it right all of the time. The private investor, thank goodness, does not have to know too much, or worry too much about it. All that really matters is getting a feel for the overall trend.

It is pointless trying to be too clever about the economy. Whatever happens, you will not understand it as well as the hosts of analysts employed in the City and around the world with nothing to do but dissect what is going on and to report on it. They are feeding information non-stop to the various investment houses. Whatever happens anywhere, someone will have a view on it, and will have analysed it long before you become aware of what is going on. In most cases, it probably does not help them much. Some never see the wood for the trees.

All that matters to the individual investor is the broad trend. You can pick up on that in a week by reading newspaper headlines, watching the TV news, being alive to what is going on around you. If homes are being re-possessed, thousands are losing their jobs, and companies are closing down, the broad trend is clear enough. Just think for yourself – basic common sense.

CONTRARY THINKING

In a way, the most important element is to understand the need for contrary thinking. This is a notion which has become so popular as almost to be hackneyed, and worn to death. But do not neglect it. Those who trumpet the value of contrarian virtues do not always give real thought to what they involve.

At base, contrary thinking is simply thinking for yourself. Observe the majority opinion, and question it. There will be times when the only sensible thing to do is to go with the masses.

They will be right, and their momentum will carry everything forward, especially in the stock market. But there will be a time when it is right to step aside.

This is crucial in relating the economy to the stock market. It is why this book is appearing now. Successful investing is about thinking ahead. When times are good, the stock market is the place for your money. But when times are getting too good, be wary. Some of the most successful investors in the world prosper by sticking to a well-worn old phrase – 'The trend is your friend'. It is well-worn because it works. The movement of the herd determines what happens to stock markets. When buyers outnumber sellers, prices go up. When sellers are most numerous, prices fall. Successful investment involves riding on those tides.

A trend is a trend until it stops being a trend. I know that sounds daft, trite nonsense. But think about it. Go with the masses while they are carrying everything their way. And then jump off when they stop. The trick is to spot when the change is going to come, and move just that little bit earlier. The small investor may not need to be quite so sharp. It may be enough to spot when the change has started, and to move in the early stages, before the trend starts running sharply in the other direction.

You do not need to be an economic genius. All you need to do is to look at the general picture. If it seems that everyone is convinced everything is wonderful, wealth and prosperity are here to stay for ever – SELL. Trouble is ahead, sure as can be. If you miss the actual turn, and find the general mood is beginning to grow more cautious while you are still hopeful, never mind – sell. You may have missed the top, but it is far safer to be out before the crunch comes.

THINKING ABOUT BUYING

When the economic scene gets so black, so grim, that people fear good times may never return – THINK about buying. As sure as can be, you are getting near the bottom.

Take note, though. While I have no hesitation in saying 'Sell' just as you think times are most wonderful, I have not suggested a definite 'Buy' when you think you have hit the bottom. Taking profits is never wrong, no matter how much extra profit you may miss. Buying at the bottom is more dangerous, because you are risking precious limited resources, and none of us can ever be certain when we have reached the bottom.

At the time of writing, there is talk of recovery. But there is also talk of a double-dip – a feeble recovery, then a renewed fall. So when you look at the economy, and the general mood is getting brighter, be careful. Let it gather pace a little. Let others have the first profits, if there are profits to be made. They will deserve them for the extra risk they are taking.

This book is written in the absolute certainty that there will be an economic recovery, and a stock market boom. Because of that, it is right to write this book now, when there are great low-price opportunities. Fine-tuning the timing is trickier. Hitting the absolute bottom is even trickier. Guaranteeing a recovery is no problem. Guaranteeing the timing is different. I offer no guarantees on that, though buying now is clearly more sensible than it was in the late eighties.

Watch for a significant, sustained fall in interest rates, and sustained inflation under 5pc. And for a more cheerful tone among the majority of commentators. Then make your move. You will have missed the first profits by waiting, but you will have increased your chances of sustained success – the kind of success which can build into significant profits.

Just one more piece of vital advice. When you do go in, remember you are at risk from the moment you give the order to buy. Read my advice on when to sell. Read it before you buy. Then read it again. And please, please, take notice of it.

CHAPTER TWO
SHOULD YOU BE IN THE STOCK MARKET?

You can make your fortune in the stock market. Be sure of it. Many people do. You do not hear much about it. They keep it quiet, sometimes even from friends and family. Every so often it hits the press. You read about an old lady who shopped at Oxfam, and left hundreds of thousands of pounds when she died. A surprised relative tells the world that she had a few shares, always liked to play the stock market. No-one dreamt she did so well.

That says a lot. It illustrates the fascination of the share game. One retired relation of mine cost his family a small fortune because he refused to consider tax planning. He wanted to keep his cash in shares. He enjoyed following the prices in the newspaper, chatting to his broker. Good luck to him. Often it is not so much about making money as having a hobby, the most consuming hobby of all. The pounds you make are points on the scoreboard.

Whether you want simply to play the game, or dream of making your fortune, it helps to know a little about the rules, what makes prices go up, and why they fall. This book is dedicated to the positive thinkers, those who want to go out and try it.

Successful share dealing can change your life. You might manage to make a real killing. Thousands of people succeed, from very modest beginnings. One of the nicest things to happen to me is when I meet or get a letter from someone who started with the help of one of my investment books, or as a result of something I wrote in the *Daily Mail*. I come across them every so often, and I am delighted. Sometimes they have done very much better using my advice than I have ever managed myself. Good luck to them.

Do not let me kid you. Most people will not make a great deal of money playing the share game. Some will get sucked in, and end up losing a lot of money. I hope that does not happen to anyone who reads this book. Heed what it says, and it will not. Be under no illusions, though. The essence of successful investment is sensible assessment of the odds. Forget this pious nonsense about responsible investment. You can gamble as madly as you like, so long as you realise that you ARE gambling madly. Just be realistic. The wilder the gamble, the longer the odds, the more likely you are to lose. It is dangerous out there. Some people should never be allowed near the stock market. There are no rules to keep them away, nothing to prevent a fool and their money being soon parted. Just try to make sure you are not one of the fools. Before you start planning that penthouse in town, the villa in Spain, and the new car you will buy with your share winnings, pause a moment. Then pause again. Share dealing can be a risky business. No matter how careful you may try to be, you can lose money at it – all of your money.

Companies do go bust, famous names among them. Investors who enjoyed astonishing gains in Polly Peck have been left with shares the tax man says are worthless (though I still have hope). Brent Walker is a debt-laden shell, Coloroll is no more, and lesser companies galore have disappeared in the recession which followed the October 1987 stock market slump. And the astonishing Maxwell affair demonstrates that even giant companies can be dominated by crooks.

When companies go bust, the shares become worthless. You lose every penny you have in them. There is no-one to complain to, no-one to blame but yourself. If you put all of your savings in a dud, you lose all of your savings.

Bad? There is worse. Many people borrow to buy shares. They put their home up as security against the loan. When it all goes wrong, they lose not just their savings, but their home as well. You would think no-one could be so stupid. They can. And if the market should enjoy a marvellous run, and you find you are making enormous profits, you may find you, too, are tempted one day. Do not laugh. You will be sucked in almost without realising it, greedy to make that much more. You would be astonished how a sudden rush of success can change the most sober-minded people into over-confident raving egotists. The warning is no joke, no cheap sensationalism. It happens. I know it. I have seen the letters, spoken to people who have done it. Once I worked with a financial journalist who got sucked into share gambling. First he sold his house, then his flat. Then he switched to a less attractive but higher paying job to keep up. He changed that, and then dropped out of sight. You would be amazed how greed can tempt people to go over the top. And then wipe them out.

You could have bought shares in Grand Metropolitan, the brewing and leisure giant, for 24p in 1974, and sold them for well over 900p in 1992. Wonderful. But what if you had paid 85p in 1974 before they fell to 24p? You would have suffered a swift, savage loss. It was brilliant if your timing was right, deadly if it was off.

You could have bought Brent Walker at under 100p, and seen it top 600p in 1989. In 1991, it touched 6p, dear at the price. The figures differ, but similar tales can be told of advertising agents Saatchi & Saatchi, and WPP. Parkfield, Roger Felber's video and engineering group – an industrial combination which ought to have sounded a few warning bells – went from wonder stock to bust inside 18 months. Polly Peck crashed to earth in 1990. John Gunn, once the City's favourite son, bombed out at British & Commonwealth. And so on, and so on.

Compile your own list. In the early nineties, it is not difficult to find crashes galore, large and small. Each one brought shattering losses to investors, people like you and I, not just faceless City giants.

It is not easy. It is not fun. The stock market can be a savage place. Each crash wrecks marriages, ruins careers, shortens lives. Legend has them diving out of windows on Wall Street during the crash of 1929. Maybe that never actually happened. But the crash blighted the lives of hundreds of thousands of Americans through the 1930s.

The Great Crash of 1987 saw one trainee accountant run up losses of over £1million in just two days, playing the option market. Thousands of traders were forced to sell their home to meet market debts. Many who were more fortunate, or perhaps more prudent, had to sell cars. Or, more painfully, were forced to take their children out of private school. Tales of little personal tragedies, not big news, were everywhere.

Playing the market is risky. Never forget it. The risks may be too great for you. Prices can turn without warning. The stock market may be too rough for you.

If you do want to play, it is simple to cut the risks down to size. Before you take the plunge, you must go through the boring basics. Everone ought to do it. Stripped down, they mean that you can only afford to play if you can afford to pay. NEVER USE MONEY YOU CANNOT AFFORD TO LOSE.

INSURANCE

Be sure about that. Do not fool yourself. Most people I know say they cannot afford to lose a penny. If that really is so, shares are not for you. In truth, though, most people with a steady job can squirrel away £1,000 or so, and use that to play, if they really want to. But, whatever you do, be sure you really want to, and really can afford to lose it. Do not cut corners to play the market.

First, if you are married, your home should be financially secure. You should be able to cover the mortgage payments comfortably each month, or pay the rent. Do take out proper insurance. A mortgage guarantee policy is essential, covering the cost of your mortgage if you should die or be unable to work through illness or disablement. Consider, too, whether you require a policy to cover your mortgage payments if you should be made redundant. Check the fine print carefully. Too many policies have terrible loopholes, letting the insurers off the hook just when you need them.

You should have general life insurance, for perhaps three or four times your annual salary. Term insurance may suit you better than an expensive endowment. Plus a pension scheme, one run by your employer, or a personal pension plan with a reputable, long-established name. By that, I mean you should only go to a company which has been established for more than 25 years.

That is a sweeping generalisation, unfair to perfectly solid newer companies. Too bad. You are not in the business of being fair. You want to be sure, above all. No matter what red tape the Government introduces to protect people, it will be far from fool-proof. Bitter experience tells me that most of us are no match for a good salesman or woman. They can make you believe almost anything they want to, and will be furious at my advice. TAKE NO NOTICE OF THEM. It is your money they want, your cash and your future which will be at risk if you buy something from someone who wants to earn a commission from convincing you.

Me? I invite nothing but complaints by offering such advice. But maybe I have learnt something. I first bought insurance more than thirty years ago. And got that wrong. A few years later, doing a show-biz interview, rock singer Screaming Lord Sutch asked me to sit in while someone tried to sell him insurance. The salesman opened a thick file of cuttings apparently praising his company. Everyone, from the *Financial Times* onwards, seemed to love it.

It sounded odd. I made some investigations around the City. Sutch, happy to say, took my advice, and never bought the insurance. The salesman was trying to sell him a Dover Plan, from the notorious company put together by Bernie Cornfeld, the American whose tag line became 'Do you sincerely want to be rich?'. It later fell apart. I refused to allow the company to advertise in the newspaper group which employed me, and returned the gifts they sent me. Many others were happy to go along with it.

The real point, though, is that you must be careful about insurance. Add up the annual premiums, and you are making a massive investment. You want your company to last for ever, to be there thirty years later. A long-established, slightly stuffy house is best. Say someone like Standard Life, or Legal & General. They may not top the performance charts short or medium term. But they will be there, giving value, when you need them.

SAVINGS

Then you need some savings put by for the legendary rainy day. It always comes, eventually. Go to somewhere boring and easily accesssible. The National Savings Investment Bank gives reasonable, rock-solid returns. Your building society is also worth-while.

Sadly, it would be nice to urge you to go to the local society which may offer a fraction of a percentage point more in interest than the nationals. Be careful. Societies do not go bust. They are always rescued by the Building Societies Association, which leans on a big brother society to take them over. But when the smaller ones hit trouble, it can take months before you can get your money out. So big might just be best.

TESSA

Rainy-day money safe, you ought to look at a TESSA. Tessas are Tax Exempt Special Savings Accounts. They allow you to save up to £9,000 free of tax, so long as you leave the money in the account for five years. You do not put it all in at once. The maximum deposit is £3,000 in year one, with up to £1,800 in years two, three, and four, leaving only £600 for year five. The rates of deposit can vary.

Interest can either be rolled up or taken out. Some accounts attract bonuses, and so on. Details vary considerably. Rates usually fall or rise in line with general rates, but there are some fixed rate offers. Watch for penalty clauses on withdrawal or transfer. If you take your money out inside five years, you lose the tax relief. For anyone intending to play the share market, a Tessa might be too restrictive. For long term savers, they are fine.

UNIT TRUSTS

The next step might be to tiptoe into the share market through a unit trust or an investment trust. Unit trusts employ managers to buy shares with the cash from investors who buy units in the trusts. The value of the units moves in line with the price of the shares the trust holds.

The idea is that a professional manager is better equipped than the individual to pick good shares, and can handle the troublesome paperwork – especially useful when it comes to investing overseas. You pay for the privilege, of course. The trusts usually take a margin of 6pc between the price you buy for and what you can sell back to the managers at. They also take an annual fee of 1pc or more.

The size of the trust rises and falls as investors buy or sell units. Each unit gives you a stake in the fund corresponding to the proportion of your investment. Most trusts have between 40 and 120 shares, so you effectively claim a tiny stake in each of 40 to 120 companies.

Because it spreads your investment, it spreads the risk of getting something badly wrong, and losing a high proportion of your cash. It also, of course, reduces the beneficial impact when the trust buys one outstandingly good investment.

Unit trusts are strictly regulated, and are solid investments. None have gone bust, even when control of the odd one has fallen into the hands of a villain. Bad managers, however, can produce poor performance, and you might find your units decline in value quite sharply. In exceptional difficult times, there could be quite long delays in being able to sell your units, though generally trusts can quickly be converted back into cash.

Respectable managers also have some poorly performing funds. Most jog along with performance just below the overall average for the sort of shares they invest in. There are more than 1,000 trusts, some of a general nature, others going for capital growth or income, and others opting for particular industries or geographical areas. They are ideal for investing overseas.

Once again, stick to the established, big name management houses. M & G, Save & Prosper, Legal & General, Fidelity, and Mercury may not always top the performance lists, but are good and reliable. Invesco MIM has a fair record, but raised eyebrows by investing in several companies associated with the chairman, Lord Stevens, once close to Robert Maxwell.

If you see a fund shrinking in size, sell it. The best performers, and those easiest to manage, are the ones which motor on steadily, or attract a flow of new money. If any fund performs badly for a year or two, do switch into something else. Managers will try to tell you that trusts are for the long term. But there is no merit in sitting for long with a poor performer. Or if you think the whole share market is going into long term decline.

Some management groups offer cash funds. Often you can switch out of a trust specialising in equities and into the cash fund at a reduced dealing cost. That makes sense when you are worried about a market setback. Check before you buy that your management group offers such a facility. As with any investment, CHECK THE WAY OUT AS YOU GO IN.

The authorities will not thank me for it, but I would be cautious about investing in any trust which is not firmly based in this country. Jersey and Isle of Man funds may be perfectly sound, but the Isle of Man in particular has a chequered financial past. Better stick to the mainland.

INVESTMENT TRUSTS

Investment trusts are an attractive alternative to unit trusts. They have a fixed share capital, and employ managers to invest that capital in a wide range of shares. The price of the investment trust shares responds to supply and demand for them in the stock market.

Obviously the better the manager does, the more valuable the fund becomes, and the greater the demand for the shares. That is the theory. In practice, for long periods most investment trust shares sell at less than the value of the shares they hold – a discount. That discount can be attractive. It generally ranges between 35pc and 10pc. It means that you can buy an investment trust share for 65p, and have 100p of money working for you. Sometimes a bidder will buy a block of shares at a discount, and try to bid for the rest with a view to selling the underlying shares, and unlocking the whole of the asset value by liquidating the trust. When it happens, that yields a useful gain to the trust shareholder.

In the early nineties, investment trust holders were helped by a strong promotional campaign which made people much more aware of investment trusts. That reduced discounts, and gave useful gains to shareholders. The same campaign, though, is pushing up management charges, which have in the past been well below those for unit trusts.

Like unit trusts, investment trusts have different objectives, some going for growth or income, particular industries, or areas of the world. Unlike unit trusts, they can invest in unquoted companies. When they get them right, they do very well. In the early nineties, however, that brought several disappointments – though there may be a useful recovery as the economy picks up.

Investment trusts can also have different classes of capital. Several attribute the dividends on all of the portfolio to a separate class of income share, while allotting most of the growth to capital shares. There are several variations. You need expert help to distinguish between them, but they can be attractive, especially for those seeking a high return.

PERSONAL EQUITY PLANS

Many unit and investment trusts offer special facilities for combining with Personal Equity Plans. These were introduced from January 1987 to encourage individual investors into the stock market, and still appear to have active Tory support. They are constantly being tinkered with, and get progressively more complicated.

They allow you to put up to £6,000 a year into a general PEP, and from January 1992 an additional £3,000 can go into a PEP investing in a single company. Provided you keep the cash in for a year, any capital gains and dividends are free of tax.

The snag is that all PEPs must have a manager. This foolish complication pops fees into City pockets, and in many cases wipes out the tax savings on the PEP. Some managers do the investment for you, others allow you to choose your own shares. Investment has to be in UK shares, unit trusts or investment trusts.

The rules change constantly. Since each investor is already allowed £5,800 of capital gains without tax, the advantages of a PEP are marginal for anyone who wants to play the market by choosing their own shares.

HOW MANY SHARES?

It is a pity that getting to share investment should involve ploughing through a mass of preparation. Heed it. Once you have followed the rules about safe financial planning, and earnt your Good Cash-Keeping Seal of Approval, you can get down to the real stock market nitty-gritty.

Do make sure the basics are right first. They may not matter for thirty or forty years. But if anything should go wrong, and you are forced to fall back on the basics, you will be grateful that you did them properly. Believe me, insurance and savings difficulties will crop up, just when you least need the worry.

There is nothing to say you need be so serious about playing the stock market. Savings and insurance are life-support systems. Shares are a diversion, an entertainment. Remember, you are only using money you can afford to lose. And you can be as brave or as barmy as you choose.

You can spend as little as £25 – say £10 for a share, and £15 dealing costs. But that would be daft. I have one share in several companies. I buy them to ensure that I receive all of the documents, and can get access to the meetings. Thankfully, *The Daily Mail* pays my dealing costs. They are not serious investments. I even get the odd computerized dividend cheque for nought pounds and nought pence.

Sometimes readers write to ask how they should split £200 between shares. Good luck to them. I never put them off. But it does not really make too much sense. If you want to make money, you ought to start with at least £1,000. If that really is too much to risk, perhaps you ought not to play. Obviously if you can manage more, so much the better. Having, say, £2,500 to split between two shares is a better bet. But if you want to try with £200, do not let me stop you. At that end of the market, you might well feel it best to go for low-priced, high-risk shares. That way, if you do get it right, you will get a decent return.

THE FUN OF IT

You can certainly treat share dealing as a game, a wild gamble. Whatever you choose. Once you start, you will enjoy the sheer fun of it (unless your first venture is a disaster). Scratch any giant industrialist, and you will find he sees making cash as part of the game, just keeping score. After, say, the first million, you do not need the money to live. You know the theme. You can only eat so many dinners each day, drive one car at a time, live in so many houses, and keep so many ladies happy five times a night.

The cash becomes squiggles on a bank statement. Does it really matter to Tiny Rowland how much he earns, or whether his Lonrho shares are worth £80m or £140m? Sir Ralph Halpern's £1m plus wage packets probably meant almost as much to him as a passport to the lists of the nation's top wage-earners as they did in hard cash terms. Never mind the humbug about press intrusion. As status symbols go, cash goes a long way. If you are not an Olympic gold athlete, attracting comment over your bulging pay packet is probably as good a public substitute for a gold medal as anything.

Similar considerations apply to the private share punter. The money is nice, but getting it right is almost nicer. The warm glow when your favourite share soars is really special, like playing Monopoly with real money. You can get the same satisfaction whether you have £50, £5,000, or £50,000 in play.

Do not be put off by any notion that you should have at least £5,000 in each share. That might be economic sense, but that is the money man talking. If you want to play for peanuts, and enjoy the game as a game, go ahead – and good luck. That way, at least, you avoid the sickening feeling that slams into your stomach when your biggest investment turns turtle. It happens, and believe me, it hurts.

CAN YOU COPE?

Above all, try to be honest about what you want from playing the stock market. And about whether you can cope emotionally, not just financially. It can be a drug, an obsession. It can take control of you, and monopolise your life. Your job and your marriage could suffer. You might end up gambling away all you can lay your hands on, getting elated when it goes well, dreadfully depressed when it turns down. I have seen it happen. Do not let the bug get you. Be sure you can control what you are doing. Decide how much you can afford to play with, and stick to it. If you lose it, let it go. Perhaps the lesson is there to be learnt – you do not have what it takes to cope with the share game. You might be surprised how serious the dangers can be. Do not shrug them off. Think carefully.

HARE OR TORTOISE?

Then you need to decide whether you are a hare, or a tortoise. Whether you are ready to take a gamble, and the risks which go with it, or would prefer to go for steady, quality shares, the kind of things which should let you sleep at nights. Are you eager for a quick profit? Or can you sit patiently waiting for gains to filter through?

There is no particular virtue in one approach or the other, though a lot of people applaud the plodder. Already, perhaps, you may have guessed that my own patience is limited. For me, the greatest investment cop-out is to concentrate on long-term performance. John Maynard Keynes, the great economist, remarked that, in the longer term, we are all dead. It is hard for me to suppress the feeling that if you are not in a share which is moving today, you have missed out. There is time enough for a slower mover tomorrow, when you have banked some profit and can afford more of a waiting game – though there are undoubtedly times when it is right to be out of the market altogether. But that should be a positive decision – dynamic, if you like, not dozy. The share game is not for sleeping.

GROWTH OR INCOME?

You need to decide, too, whether you are after capital growth or income. The two are not mutually exclusive. This book is biased towards the seeker after capital growth, where the real fun and action is. If you want income, perhaps an insurance-linked guaranteed growth bond, or government securities might suit you better than shares. If you want income with some capital growth, look at a high income investment trust or unit trust, linked to a Personal Equity Plan.

Patience, though, is vital, especially to a share beginner. Choosing a steady share allows you time to learn what is going on. No-one will learn much from one which doubles or halves in a fortnight. That will be down to beginner's luck, good or bad. Months spent watching prices will give you a feel about an individual share, and how it behaves in different market moods. That can pay off later.

The amount of time and effort you put into watching investments will help determine how you invest. Ideally, the cautious investor will want to watch long and hard, perhaps opting for make-believe investments, tracking them on paper before actually buying. The careful investor also spreads the risk, splitting cash between shares so that one loser does not drag the whole portfolio down too far.

TAKING A GAMBLE

Others will hope to spot special situations, and plunge the lot on them. Spreading your risk may be safer, but it waters down the benefits of a big winner. Finding just one big one is difficult enough. When you are convinced you have it, you may want to leap in, all or nothing. That strategy attracts little support among City investment advisers. Every time, they opt for the slow, steady route. That way, the adviser is proof against accusations of irresponsibility. In appearing to guard your back, he is also guarding his own – one of the first principles of City conduct. It is your money – make your own rules. But think about it first.

In practice, many first-time investors are looking for an out-and-out punt. The last thing they want is some boring name from the glorious past of British industry, paying a predictable dividend that barely keeps pace with inflation. Many such stocks have come under terrible pressure in the early nineties. And they would never suit the kind of players who want to treat the Stock Exchange as a glorified casino. There is nothing against that. Put all of your cash on the red if you wish. Just understand what you are doing. If you lose the lot, there is no-one to blame but yourself.

SOMEONE ELSE KNOWS MORE

If you win, hallelujah. Just do not get carried away by it. Never believe that you have found the winning formula. That is a way to disaster. One winner and you will be entering the most testing time of your new-found career. You will know just enough to think you can do it – but not remotely enough to understand that you will never know quite enough. Be sure. Someone, somewhere always knows more than you do. The American insider trading scandal revealed ace market player Ivan Boesky as merely the spider at the centre of a web of privileged information, a cheat buying knowledge illegally. We have our own mini-Boeskys, make no mistake. They understand the market better than you, they can get more information than you, and they know far better how to use it. They will gobble you up if ever you cross their path.

EVERYONE HAS AN ANGLE

Cynical? Perhaps. But cynicism is an essential tool for every investor. There is very little certain about investment – but you can be absolutely sure that everyone you deal with has an angle.

Brokers want to earn commission from doing your trades, to feed on what you know. Bankers want to earn from you, lend you money. Tip sheets want you to subscribe to them, and some may have other reasons for recommending the shares they do. Company directors want you to believe in them so that you will help promote their shares. Investment authors want you to buy their books. And so on.

The angle might suit you very well, might do you good if everyone is pulling in the same direction to get the share price higher. Often the angles will be too well concealed for you to spot them. But they will be there. Always ask yourself what is in it for you – and for the other fellow? That is a crucial investment rule.

CHAPTER THREE
WHERE TO START

There is very little you need to know if you want to invest in the stock market: the name of a share to buy, the name of a bank, stockbroker, building society or share shop to buy it for you, and how to write the cheque to pay for – not even that, really. Most of the brokers I know would be happy to take used fivers in a carrier bag.

The virgin investor can score by luck alone. One newspaper proved it by opening the back pages of the *Financial Times* and throwing darts. This 'Bull's Eye Portfolio' beat one picked by City worthies, supposedly skilled in the art of share selection. Goodness knows what happened to the shares picked by the newspaper's own tipsters.

Of course, you are just as likely – rather more likely – to come an absolute cropper by relying on luck alone. Or perhaps by kidding yourself that you do have a little understanding. That can be lethal. We all get it wrong sometimes. It takes real application to search out a whole portfolio of obscure non-starters. Yet some apparently sensible people manage it, usually with the prompting of some share pushing telephone adviser, a new friend who assures them he can put them on to a winner. And then churns them in and out of a succession of duds. I shudder when it get the letters. Happily, I have helped close down a few of the villains.

These days, too, there are many people with a tidy little portfolio made up of privatisation issues. Most have done reasonably well. Share trading looks simple and relatively low-risk to such folk. Do not be fooled. When the Government wants to rig the market in your favour, it can. Privatisations are the exceptions. Most investments do not work that way. Most of the time, the market is slanted heavily against the small player, and leaning more that way each day.

Do not let it put you off. Just be alive to the reality. Once that is understood, you only really need to know as much about the City and share investment as you feel you want to. You are never likely to master it all. After thirty years of financial journalism, I am way short. Every so often, I make terrible misjudgements. And I keep stumbling across things I never knew, and things that I will never understand. It does me good, I tell myself. If ever I should think I understand it all, next stop the nut-house – or the work house.

If you want to play your hunches, back the tips you get at your local, or from your favourite newspaper, good luck. It might work. Nothing in my book says you cannot or should not take a gamble, so long as you can afford it.

The more you know about what you are doing, though, the more comfortable you should be. And it will be more fun. Certainly a working knowledge of the stock market will swing the investment odds in your favour.

Try to be realistic about it. Your knowledge and experience will be limited, but you may be able to see things others do not – or you may simply get lucky.

It is easy to be intimidated by the City. The air of mystery and tradition, money and power, spiced with a dash of the old school tie and the gentleman's club can appear distinctly off-putting. The atmosphere lingers on despite the overseas invasion which followed the change in Stock Exchange rules in the Big Bang of October 1986. But the rise of the meritocracy and the computer-literate number-crunchers has not killed off all of the old ways. The odd top hat still surfaces, and one or two magnificently sombre wood-panelled offices survive to house the senior partners – though these days they are often old rooms transported to nasty new buildings. A man in a pink frock-coat still guards the doors of the Bank of England.

The splendid tradition may cling on, gently emphasising the divisions between them and us. They, it appears, are steeped in generations of money matters, born with an inherent understanding of such things. The rest of us may try, but can never attain quite the same eminence.

Do not fall for it. There are brilliant minds in the City. Sometimes they make the most remarkable mistakes. There are fewer fifth generation fools than there used to be, but some survive. Alongside them are hundreds of thousands of ordinary people doing ordinary jobs, as liable as all of us to get a little muddled now and then.

In a way, the most intimidating aspect now is the techno-flash reliance on computers and figures. The so-called 'rocket scientists' who devise computer programmes to determine the value of this, that and the other are way beyond my comprehension.

It does not matter. Sometimes it becomes clear for all to see that what they are doing does not amount to a row of beans. They may make a fortune for themselves and their companies. But every so often, it goes badly wrong. In the real world, there are so many variables that sometimes it is impossible to reduce all of them to arithmetical formulae. Reality sometimes swipes them from behind. The figures may look right, but the answer is all wrong. More than once I have heard about some elaborate programme which guarantees a sure-fire profit. It always works – until it smashes into that freak, one in a million chance. Then everyone is wiped out.

Then there are the people who shade the truth, all the way from little white lies to grim black crookery and thievery. Events at the Lloyd's insurance market and recent court cases may have made it appear that the City is full of con-men, simply concerned with robbing everyone blind. It is not so. Most of the City is tolerably honest. But business is business.

BE SURE IT MAKES SENSE

What really matters to you is whether the things you are concerned with make sense to you. Nothing else counts. IF YOU DO NOT UNDERSTAND IT, DO NOT DO IT.

Money men have an angle. They want to sell you something. They may be leading you up the garden path, they may be lost themselves, or they may be guiding you to investment heaven. But if you cannot follow every step of the way, forget it. Never hesitate to ask them to slow down, go back, and start again. The instant you get lost, stop them – and make them explain it all over again.

NEVER, NEVER, NEVER, LET ANYONE BLIND YOU WITH FIGURES. NEVER BE AFRAID TO APPEAR AN ABSOLUTE IDIOT. If you do not understand, keep asking until you do. If you cannot get to grips with it (this applies especially to choosing the insurance raised earlier) you have found your answer. It is not for you.

Trust yourself. You will be the loser if you get it wrong. If you allow yourself to be blinded by jargon that you do not understand, but did not query for fear of looking foolish, who is the real fool? It will be you, and it will be your money that has gone.

Do not hesitate. Of course there will be things that you will genuinely be unable to understand. Nothing wrong with that. Leave them to the experts.

And there will things you will not quite be able to grasp because that is exactly what is meant to happen. Respectable City houses spend a great deal of time and trouble over the way their documents are worded. Often they have drafts galore, considered carefully by comittees. and changed again and again. Sentences are rarely sloppily worded by mistake, rarely obscure without a reason. If there is something which does not quite seem right to you, you may well have spotted the flaw which the wording was intended to conceal, to gloss over.

Do not feel stupid if you do not understand. You may be slow on the uptake. Or you may be quite the opposite. You may have spotted the catch.

Above all, the investment game should be simple common sense. STICK TO WHAT YOU UNDERSTAND. Ask the questions which seem sensible to you – and make sure you get answers you feel comfortable with. Otherwise, walk away.

THE LANGUAGE OF THE MARKET

Any sensible investor will recognise, of course, that you need to be able to understand the basics before you can ask the right questions. If some of the vocabulary seems off-putting, do not worry. You will grow used to it. If some of the arithmetic appears a problem, never mind. You rarely need do the sums yourself. You can almost always find the answer somewhere, or get someone to provide it. Most of the answers are readily available – in newspapers, investment magazines, and on the electronic information services which your stockbroker or banker should have at their fingertips.

If calculating a price earnings ratio sounds tricky, look it up, or ask someone. It is in the share price table carried by many leading newspapers. What matters about the price earnings ratio – as in all City sums – is what it tells you, not whether you can work it out yourself.

WHAT IS A SHARE?

What is a share? Easy. Exactly what it says. A share is a piece of paper which represents a part of a business. Say four people get together. and each puts £25 into a business. That company will have £100 capital invested in it. Each of the four investors will have one quarter of the business. They can slice the shares up any way they wish – each of the four can have one £25 share, or 25 shares of £1, or 50 shares of 50p. And so it goes. All public companies work roughly that way, but bigger. They have millions of shares, each one entitling the holder to one equal part of the company. The more shares you have, the bigger your stake in the company.

People frequently use 'stocks' and 'shares' interchangeably. Strictly speaking, stocks are securities which earn a fixed rate of interest, whereas dividends on shares can rise and fall. Some shares are actually called stock units. Technically, for example, ICI does not have shares, but £1 stock units. There is no practical difference between them and £1 shares in other companies. Stocks or shares, it does not really matter.

NOMINAL VALUE

British Telecom is one of our biggest public companies. It has shares with a nominal value of just 25p each. Nominal, or par, value does not matter much. It is simply the face value a company choses to put on the shares – an accounting convention. In UK companies, nominal value is usually between 1p and £1. All UK companies, by law, must have a nominal value, though American companies often have shares with no par value.

A company can just as easily issue capital of £100,000 in 100,000 shares with a par value of £1 each as it can 10,000,000 shares with 1p par value. The par or nominal value means nothing in itself. A share with a 1p nominal value is not necessarily worth 1p, just as a share with £1 nominal value may not be worth £1. Shares are worth what someone will pay for them – the market price – and nothing else.

Do not be put off good shares because they have a par value of say, 5p, and a price of 120p. Conversely, do not think you have found a bargain by paying 5p for a share with a nominal value of £1. In practice, the main significance of par or nominal value lies in calculating what dividend you actually get.

DIVIDENDS

Dividends are the equivalent to the rate of interest you get on your share. They are usually described as so many pence per share, or expressed as a percentage of the nominal (or par) value of the shares. A 10 per cent dividend means you are paid 10p a share on shares with a nominal value of £1. If your shares have a nominal value of 10p, then the 10 per cent dividend is worth 1p a share. It is just an arithmetical device, nothing more.

Most shares are called Ordinary shares (or equities), and produce dividends that are decided by the board of directors. Broadly speaking, these rise or fall as profits rise or fall, though there is no set rule. Dividends are normally paid twice a year, usually as an interim dividend (normally the smaller payment), and as a final dividend (often larger, and set after the profits for the full year are known). There is often quite a long delay – sometimes months – between dividends being announced and the actual cheques being sent to shareholders.

FIXED INTEREST CAPITAL

Companies have several forms of capital other than Ordinary shares. Most are paid a fixed rate of dividend, or interest. As compensation, they usually have first claim on profits, so their dividend can be viewed as safer than Ordinary dividends. If a company goes bust, normally the fixed interest capital will have a greater claim on the assets than the Ordinary shares, so fixed interest holders stand a better chance of getting something back. Fixed interest capital is normally most attractive to those seeking higher income, and can be ignored for capital gains purposes in normal circumstances, though I touch later on capital growth opportunities. The most widely traded forms of fixed interest capital are preference stocks, loan stocks, and convertible loan stocks.

CONTRACT NOTES AND SHARE CERTIFICATES

As soon as your broker or banker tells you they have bought, you are the legal owner of your shares. The City's motto is 'My word is my bond'. Although that bond may sometimes look a little grubby, the system honours it. The contract note is what you get from your broker or banker giving the details of what has been bought or sold, the price, and the commission and other charges. It is legal proof of ownership, so you need to keep it safe. You will have to refer to it when compiling your capital gains table for your tax return.

A few weeks later, you will be sent a share certificate by the registrars acting for the company whose shares you have bought. Ask your broker or banker to chase it up if it does not arrive within two months.

NO MATTER WHAT they say, DO NOT let your broker or banker register your shares in a nominee account – though certain PEP accounts may force you to bend on this. Make sure the shares are registered in your name, and insist on getting the certificate. Some firms will give you impressive-sounding reasons for registering the shares in their nominee name. It may sound fine, until things go wrong. If they do, you will regret not having the certificate yourself, believe me.

Some day, share certificates may be abolished. The Stock Exchange has been blundering around for years with a computer-based system called Taurus.

THE COMPANY CALENDAR

Each company has a calendar, dates on which it makes big set-piece announcements through the year. The most important cover the interim profit statement, and the preliminary results for the full year.

You cannot count on either of these crucial statements being sent to you as a shareholder. Though most companies post a copy of their interim statement to shareholders, it goes out several days after the contents have been announced to the Stock Exchange. In theory, all investors should be treated equally. Companies are not allowed to give advance knowledge of any significant announcements to anyone.

Impeccable as the theory may be, the practice is very different. Some investors are more equal than others, and have gained in influence since Big Bang in 1986. Company announcements are sent first to a Stock Exchange department. There they are checked, processed, and flashed around the City on sophisticated and costly electronic communications systems. All of the big investment houses, the brokers and such, have them. So the City gets any company news the instant it is released, and can buy and sell long before the small shareholder gets a whiff of what is happening.

Individual investors have to wait, and wait. The Oracle system available on Teletext TV screens speeds access up a little, but it is a poor substitute for the City screens. The expensive 0898 telephone systems are way behind. The whole unsatisfactory system may shortly become even more confused. In the name of greater competition, the Government has ruled that company announcements should now also be sent to news systems which compete with the Stock Exchange. In some cases, this may allow a different set of subscribers the first bite at sensitive information, and could even open the system to hoax announcements.

Almost all company news items are sent to the newspapers, though increasingly bad news is not always fully circulated, or is sent late in the day when papers might miss it. Whatever happens, there is no guarantee that news of your company will appear. The *Daily Mail*, for example, comments only on what it considers the most interesting items. The *Financial Times* publishes almost everything, sometimes two or three days late. For the private investor, it is hit or miss. Only in the unusual event of a company posting news overnight, and delaying any announcement until the start of share dealings on the following morning is there anything like equal access to information.

INTERIM REPORTS

When you get your interim report, it will carry an estimate of profits for the first half of the trading year, plus the amount of any interim dividend. There may also be a short comment on progress. Most of the news will have been forecast by stockbrokers who follow the company, so the City knows what to expect. Only a real surprise will move the share price much. Quite often, prices fall on good news. It will have been anticipated by the City backroom boys who bought ahead of the figures. Unless there is something extra special, they will have taken their profits well before any news reaches you.

In practice, many companies also quietly tip off their City friends. It is considered bad form to surprise your big shareholders. Tiny Rowland did it early in 1992, and attracted a terrible fuss when Lonrho cut the dividend, even though over half the City had hated him for two decades.

If a company finance director sees City expectations are out of line, someone will quietly ring the company's brokers. Or maybe there will be a cosy dinner or lunch. A nod and a wink will ensure that the real position is conveyed.

I was horrified to spot a blatant example of this at ultra-respectable Tate & Lyle, the sugar giant, with brokers gently downgrading profit forecasts just a fortnight after the annual meeting.

The company had let some brokers know of a few problems, without a word to the mass of shareholders at the annual meeting – the ideal time to do it.

Brokers often submit their own profit forecasts to companies – just as a matter of courtesy and to see that they have not made any silly mistakes, you understand. Companies can then nudge the forecasts into position. Do the brokers and their privileged clients buy or sell as a result of this sort of information? You bet they do.

Quite how this nod-and-a-wink fiddle squares with treating all investors equally is beyond me. Some companies do not do it. But most play this not-quite-insider game. You are a small shareholder? Too bad, old chap.

PRELIMINARY PROFITS

The most important announcement is that of preliminary profits for the year. It is not usually sent to investors, because it is normally followed a few weeks later by the report and accounts. They are called 'preliminary' profits because they may technically not be fully certified by the auditors, though there is unlikely to be any further change. The full report and accounts can be anything from a slim 20 page black and white job to a glossy affair with 60 pages or more, full of colour photographs. There may be a statement of company philosophy, and perhaps a few special offers of cut-price company products. Glossiness does not necessarily denote investment merit. It may mean quite the opposite.

THE ANNUAL MEETING

The accounts must carry at least three weeks' notice of the time and place of the annual meeting. All Ordinary shareholders are entitled to attend, ask questions, and vote on half a dozen routine proposals. You can vote even if you do not go along. Companies must send out proxy cards, allowing you to post your vote if you wish. In most companies, there is one vote for each share.

The votes will normally cover the election or re-election of a few directors (some stand for re-election every few years), and will probably seek permission to issue new shares without consulting shareholders. There will be a motion approving payment of the dividend, and allowing the board to decide the pay of the auditors – daft, since the auditors in theory report to the shareholders, not the board.

The chairman may well say something about current trading. Sometimes that will be circulated to shareholders, and to the press. But if you skip the meeting, you may miss whatever has been said.Usually, it will not be of great consequence. Just sometimes, though, there is high drama. Many companies post their final dividend cheques a few days after the annual meeting. Remember, as a shareholder the theory is that you own a piece of the company, and the directors are employed to manage it on behalf of the shareholders. If you do not like the way things are being done, you are entitled to write to the chairman and tell him so. Sensible letters deserve sensible replies. Usually they get them. If they do not, there is little you can do, except sell your shares – or, in extreme cases, tell the *Daily Mail*. In practice, individual shareholders are something of a nuisance, to be tolerated. But most companies have the sense to go through the motions. And some really do care.

CHAPTER FOUR
WHY SHARES RISE AND FALL

Share prices rise because there are more buyers than sellers. They fall when there are more sellers than buyers. That is the standard, half-mocking City reply to the classic question about why shares move. The chap giving the answer has no more idea of what is really going on than the questioner. His answer is correct, but it tells you very little. He does not want to reveal his ignorance, so in grand City style, bundles it up in a bit of a joke – suits a lot of City chaps, you might think, a bit of a joke.

Quite often, though, you can unearth no better explanation. Share prices frequently appear to move for no reason, pure chance. In reality, that is not so. There is always a reason. It may not be terribly significant. But you do not know it.

Do not get caught like the City smarties. ADMIT YOUR IGNORANCE to yourself. No good pretending you know something you do not, then risking your money on it.

Perhaps much of the change was due largely to chance of a sort. The people who actually change share prices are the market-makers, the City's share wholesalers. Before Big Bang, they used to be called jobbers, and worked rather differently. Now there are as many as 15 market-makers in some shares, all agreeing to set prices and buy or sell quantities of that share. The prices they will trade at appear on screens throughout the City, with an indication of the number of shares for which the listed prices hold good. For larger deals, they are entitled to change their prices. Each one watches the competition, and moves his prices in accordance with what his rivals are doing. In most stocks, there are two or three leading market-makers, who set the trends which most others follow. So they play follow-my-leader.

It could be that the leading market-maker in one share decided he was not generating enough business. So he knocked the price down to see if he could attract buyers. The other market-makers might follow him down. To keep his price advantage, the first one might cut again.

The price has fallen. From the outside, it looks as if something must have happened. But it has not. It may even be that no shares have changed hands. The story will rarely be quite as simple as that, but it could be – especially in the shares of smaller companies, where there are only two or three market-makers, and one is dominant.

Sometimes the price could change for reasons which appear to make even less sense. Perhaps the market-maker had a bad morning – he could not finish the Times crossword, the train was late again, and he tripped leaving the lift. In a foul mood, he sees the pound looking weak, so he lowers the price of all of the shares he makes markets in, just in case something happens. After lunch, he feels better, and the pound is steadier. Since no-one has come in to buy and give him business at his lower prices, he leaves them where they are. His bad mood could have wiped millions of pounds off the share value of the companies concerned, for no real reason. Too bad.

It may seem grossly unfair to the small investor, hanging on every move in price. The company may be trading better and better, but the shares are drifting down. The two things are not necessarily linked. It is no good complaining. NO-ONE EVER SAID THE CITY HAD TO BE FAIR.

My first investment book was called *How to Make A Killing In the Share Jungle*. I chose the title carefully. It IS a jungle for small investors. All too often they get gobbled up because they think there are clear rules which everyone plays by. Forget it. Self-interest is the only rule which is honoured consistently.

SELF-INTEREST RULES, OK?

Self-interest explains the kind of general move which often costs private investors dearly when the market is dull. Trying to generate some interest in trading, market-makers frequently lower prices when business is quiet, and the mood depressed. They also reduce the number of shares they are ready to trade at their listed prices. It makes sense. Most market-makers will actually be holding some shares. They make their money from the difference between the price at which they buy, and the price for which they sell. Any shares they actually hold ties up money, often borrowed money. If they can shift shares quickly by making a small cut in prices, they will, especially if the market is falling. The quicker they trade shares on, the less interest they pay on their borrowings, and the less danger of being caught out by a big fall if the market is hit by bad news.

At other uncertain times, they cut prices in the hope of avoiding having to buy more shares – unless they see the chance of selling quickly at a profit. So in dull periods, the instinct is always to lower prices and trade in fewer shares. If depression hangs around for some time, prices can be marked down gently but regularly. In smaller company shares, that can mean savage falls over, say, three months, without any change in the underlying fortunes of the company. Or many shares actually being sold.

The reverse tends to happen, of course, in good times. Market-makers are quick to raise prices when demand is good, so they can take a bigger margin between what they buy for and the price they sell at. Few shareholders complain about the laws of the jungle then.

On top of all of this, of course, there are all kinds of games between tough traders competing in a business where large amounts of money change hands. Stockbrokers are always trying to guess how many shares the market-makers actually hold. If, for example, it appears that market-makers are short of stock (do not hold much) they could be caught out by a rush of buying. Because market-makers are obliged to deal in the size and price they quote on their screens, they could be forced to sell shares they do not have. If that happens, they will try to raise prices sharply, to encourage people to sell to them quickly, and fill the hole. Otherwise they might find prices are forced still higher against them, and eventually have to pay much more to buy the shares they have promised to deliver.

There are many variations on this theme. Sometimes market-makers will set prices sharply lower, especially if there has been a buying rush in a particular share. They will be hoping short-term gamblers will panic and sell. And that is without touching on what many feel often become wholesale attempts at manipulation by some houses.

No way to run a stock market, wiping millions off the value of public companies because of nasty little games among the professionals? Crazy and irresponsible? Perhaps. Obviously the system is imperfect. It always has been. It is getting worse. The individual investor cannot hope to keep pace with all that goes on. If you are going to play, resign yourself to the inevitable. There is always the chance that you will get caught out by some price move which appears absolutely illogical. The unexpected is always lurking in the background, ready to catch you out.

WHAT OUGHT TO MAKE PRICES MOVE

Do not get discouraged. There are certain fairly clearly defined basic factors which influence prices. You can get by without knowing them all, but it is as well to have some idea. Since

PLAYING THE STOCK MARKET IS ULTIMATELY ABOUT ANTICIPATING WHAT OTHER INVESTORS WILL DO, and using it to your advantage, it makes sense to be aware of the sort of rules they are using. No rule is absolutely reliable, and it may not always have the impact you expect. Give it a little thought, and you can turn many of the rules on their head – a sort of game of bluff, and double-bluff.

In the end, though, it is simple. You want to buy shares in a company which is doing well, and will do better. Rising profits generate increased dividends which attract investors who seek higher income. Along the way, that brings capital gains.

It is difficult to know where to start if you are trying to assess how well a company may be placed. Each year, every company must send out an annual report and accounts. It is of limited value, because it is largely historical, a fuzzy snapshot of what the company looked like on the final day of the last trading year. Share prices are all about what is going to happen next. But studying the past gives you a firm base, a starting point, and can yield valuable clues to the future. Even if you are not a shareholder, most companies will send you a copy of their most recent accounts, if you write to the company secretary at the registered office.

The report and accounts is split in to seven main sections; the chairman's statement; the directors' report; the profit and loss account; the balance sheet; the statement of the source and application of funds; the auditors' report; the notes.

THE CHAIRMAN'S STATEMENT

The chairman's statement may be accompanied by a separate report from the managing director, or chief executive (usually simply different titles for the chap who actually runs the company). Some companies publish reports from managers of individual sectors of the business. These may provide an idea of how things look in the current year, and perhaps a useful feel of what the company actually does. Note the names of the operating companies (there is usually a full list near the back of the report). Often the names bear little relationship to the name on your share certificate. Great Universal Stores, for example, owns Burberrys, Times Furnishing, and mail order giants like Marshall Ward. Did you realise that Hanson owns Imperial Tobacco and London Brick? If you identify the actual operating companies, you may see them around, and be better able to judge what is going on in the company as a whole.

THE DIRECTORS' REPORT

The directors' report deals briefly with what the company does, outlines changes in structure – e.g. sales or purchases of major parts of the business – and lists how many shares the directors own (have a beneficial interest in), and how many they look after as trustees (non-beneficial). It will also show what options they have to buy shares. It should also show any changes since the previous accounts, and may detail moves between the end of the year and publication of the report. In addition, it should list anyone holding more than 3pc of the shares.

Obviously it is worth checking to see what the directors have been doing with their shares, and whether they control the company. A holding of 50pc or more clearly gives them complete control, but over 30pc can usually be regarded as effective control. A holding of this size diminishes the chances of a hostile takeover bid, unless some outsider also has 29.9 pc – which means a bid could be in the offing. If there are several outsiders with more than 3pc, or someone is building up a share stake, there is more chance of a bid.

THE PROFIT AND LOSS ACCOUNT

People often confuse the profit and loss account and the balance sheet. The p and l deals with how the company has traded through the year, and whether it has made any money. The balance sheet shows what the company owns and had available to use to make that money.

All of the p and l figures show a comparison with the previous trading period, which gives a crude indication of how the fortunes of the company have been moving. Obviously, a rising trend is encouraging, but is is important to check the notes to see that there have been no exceptional factors to influence any change. Most items have a number next to them, indicating which note gives further details.

The p and l account shows how the profit or loss for the last trading year was made up. The top line is usually turnover or sales (effectively the same thing). Then comes the cost of sales – a hefty figure that covers all the normal costs of running a business. If it rises by a smaller proportion than sales, then there is a bigger increase in the next line, the trading (or gross) profit.

What comes next varies. It may be the share of profits or losses from related companies – businesses the main company does not own completely. Part of their profit will have to be knocked off the main company's total, because this belongs to the other shareholders in that business. If the partly owned companies made losses, there will be a credit to the main company, representing the share of losses to be borne by outside shareholders. These items are often called minority interests. There may also be an item for other expenses. That may include staff costs and depreciation. The depreciation represents a figure knocked off each year for wear and tear on premises, machinery, fittings and such. In theory, it is set aside to cover the cost of replacing these items when they are worn out.

Then there will be a line showing interest charges or credits. And perhaps the contribution to the employee profit-sharing scheme, if such exists. Below that, you have pre-tax profit, the figure most widely quoted by the press.

It is not the most important figure. Net profit, struck after paying tax and meeting any dividends on preference capital (if there is any), fills that role. Because of capital allowances, past losses, profits in low tax areas, and so on, the tax charge might well be below the figure you might normally expect. There is always some debate over whether analysts should apply a theoretical full tax charge so that they can compare like with like when looking at different companies. Nowadays, however, general practice is to take whatever the company says, leaving perhaps a query in the back of your mind.

Net profits show what is available to pay dividends, and the next line in the accounts often gives the actual cost of paying whatever dividend the directors recommend. In practice, dividends do not always cost what accounts say, but that need not bother you. What is left after paying dividends is available to be transferred to reserves, where it can be used to expand the business. The bigger the reserves, the better, so long as shareholders get a decent dividend.

Some companies then show earnings per share, one of the most widely used figures in the investment world. This is calculated by dividing the profits after tax and preference dividends (sometimes known as net profits attributable to Ordinary shareholders) by the number of Ordinary shares in issue. Be careful. Issued capital will be listed in the notes, but do distinguish between authorised capital (how many shares the company could issue) and issued capital (how many shares it has actually issued).

Take an example of how to calculate earnings per share (widely abbreviated to eps). Assume that after tax and preference dividends, the company has net profits of £500,000, and it has one million shares in issue. That company has earnings per share of 50p. Divide earnings per share into the share price, and you arrive at the price earnings ratio. Say the shares sell at 450p, the price earnings ratio would be 9 (450p divided by 50p).

The price earnings ratio – often simply called the p e ratio – is the most widely used of all investment measurements. Sometimes it is expressed in different ways – people talk about a share selling at so many times earnings, or so many years' earnings. It is the same old p e ratio. Effectively it shows you how many years it would take the company to earn net profits equal to the stock market value of the company.

You will not find the p e ratio in the annual report. It would be misleading to put it there, because it depends on the share price, which is liable to change at any moment. As the shares rise, the p e rises. As they fall, so the pe ratio falls.

THE BALANCE SHEET

The next major section of the report and accounts is the balance sheet. This displays what the company owned and owed on the last day of the trading year (companies can choose their own dates for trading years). The assets are listed first. There are fixed assets; land, buildings, plant and machinery, and so on.

Next come current assets; investments, stocks, cash, and debtors (the money owed to the company). The bigger the assets, the better. Check the date on which the fixed assets were last valued. Though the slump of the late eighties and early nineties has caused problems, it could be that the true value of property is understated if there has not been a revaluation in recent years.

Look at plant, machinery and stock values still more sceptically. Outdated plant and machinery may not be saleable at the balance sheet value, and if a company gets caught with a lot of stock that has declined in value, that is a problem. A higher stock position could well be bad news, rather than good. Perhaps the company is struggling to sell what it makes. That will nearly always be accompanied by a rise in the overdraft.

There will also be a figure for creditors, covering money the company has to pay out within a year. This could include overdrafts, and possibly tax bills. Subtract creditors from current assets, and you get net current assets – or net current liabilities if short term debts exceed the quickly realisable assets.

Next the balance sheet adds fixed assets and net current assets (or takes away net current liabilities). Then it subtracts other liabilities – the money the company owes but does not have to repay for a year or more. These generally include large loans that run for a fixed number of years before repayment. Take one from the other, and you have the net asset value of the business, the price you would, in theory, get if you shut up and sold out. The greater the excess of assets over liabilities, the richer the company, especially if assets are strong in cash or saleable property. Be careful, though. Strong asset value might not always indicate a healthy company. If a high proportion of the value is in fixed assets which might not easily be sold, the business could run out of cash – especially if there are large fixed loans which must be repaid in the near future.

Beneath this is a section showing how it is all financed, through capital and reserves. There will be the amount of paid-up share capital, covering the preference shares and Ordinary shares in issue, at their nominal value. Then there are reserves, the sums left over through the years from profits after tax and dividends. Put them together, and they are known as shareholders' funds.

Increasingly, investors are coming to appreciate the importance of not allowing debt to grow too high, and so they watch the proportion of debt to shareholders' funds. That is called gearing. The higher the gearing, or the proportion of borrowing, the more investors worry. It means the company will have to earmark much more revenue to pay out interest, leaving less for dividends and for growth. And there is the worry of how that debt is eventually going to be paid back.

If a company hits trouble, gearing assumes particular importance. Loans are usually extended under elaborate agreements with the lenders, dictating that the loans must be repaid if certain ratios are hit. Though such details are not made public, they can be vital. The lenders will always have a claim on company assets before anything is repaid to investors.

SOURCE AND APPLICATION OF FUNDS

All accounts carry a page dealing with the source and application of funds. This shows where the cash has come from through the year, and where it went. Coming in, there will be profits, depreciation, asset sales, and new borrowings or share issues. Going out, there will be the cost of dividends, tax, and buying companies. Obviously it is better to see more cash coming in than going out. Using this with the balance sheet notes can often give you a clearer idea of what is actually happening. You really want to see as much cash as possible generated from trading.

THE AUDITORS' REPORT

Somewhere in the whole shebang will be a modest, but vital, section – the auditors' report. Normally this is a few brief lines, certifying that the financial statements give a true and fair view of the state of affairs, and conform to the Companies Act. A glance will suffice if that is the message. It will be for most companies. If it differs, watch out.

Strictly speaking, the auditors are accountants employed by the shareholders to verify that the directors are running the business in accordance with the Companies Act, and that the figures in the report and accounts are what they say they are. There is considerable debate over just what this means, and in recent years, auditors have been encouraged to blow the whistle if they stumble across fraud. In reality, auditors interpret their responsibilities in limited fashion, and can be persuaded to accept all sorts of practices which normal people would consider outrageous.

There are strong moves to tighten up on audits. They may produce results. But it would be foolish to expect too much. It would certainly be wrong to suggest that a determined board could not persuade auditors to agree to practices which some might consider unusual, and wrong to suggest that they could not be fooled completely by a determined crook.

So do not place too much faith in a clean audit report. Most companies which go bust have one in their last accounts. In the rare cases when auditors signal something is wrong, they do it in a stilted code. The accounts are normally presented on a going-concern basis, which means things are fine. If there is any qualification to that phrase, it can be serious.

The auditors may, for example, say that continued operation as a going concern is dependent on further finance, or on the continuation of existing support from bankers. That means the company has run out of money, and could go bust if anyone asks for their loans back. If the auditors are unable to form an opinion as to whether the accounts give a true and fair view, sell at once. They are telling you something is badly wrong.

Almost any qualification is serious, but one or two can be shrugged aside. Sometimes companies do not conform to some recommended accounting rule, and the auditors are obliged to draw attention to it. They may agree that it does not matter. If so, they will say that the accounts give a true and fair view, subject to the variation.

One further point; check who the auditors are, and where they are based. Big names are by no means infallible, and there may be a potential conflict of interest if another part of the same accounting firm is supplying business advice services to the company whose accounts they are auditing. But smaller accounting firms may be more vulnerable to pressure from companies if they do not have other big name audit duties. Directors do lean on auditors, and auditors do sometimes bend. Watch out, too, if some regional branch of a big name accountant is doing the audit on a major company. Local politics may play a part in that one.

THE NOTES

Many of the really interesting items in company accounts can be unearthed from the notes. These add a certain amount of the detail to the big figures up front. Before you get into them, read the statement of accounting policies carefully. Later in the book, dealing with creative accounting, I cover some of the tricks to watch for. One useful preliminary check, though, is to get the accounts for the year before. Compare the two statements, and look for changes. Do not imagine that a word here or there does not matter. It does.

If you spot the smallest alteration, make every effort to see what it could mean. Nine times out of ten, it WILL be of consequence. These days, it will often mean that the board has found some way of presenting the figures in a slightly more flattering – or less damaging – light.

Scanning the fine print of the notes is well worthwhile. In the initial stages, you may well feel you have had more than enough from ploughing through the main parts of the report and accounts. Fair enough. As time goes by, you will appreciate what nuggets there are in the notes.

DEPRECIATION

This is a regular source of interest. It can be vital. Take two transport companies. Company one may write down the cost of lorries over four years, or 25pc a year, setting aside a quarter of their cost against profits. Company two may write lorries off over five years, or 20pc a year. Of course, company one may be able to run the lorries for five years. If their value has been written down to nil after four years, no depreciation will need to be set aside against profits in year five. Profits benefit significantly. Company two will have shown higher profits in years one to four, but will still be writing the lorries off in year five. So company two should have lower profits in that year.

In the real world, things are not that simple. But you can see the scope for flexibility. One regular source of such accounting speculation has been the way security companies use depreciation. Late in 1991, I began to focus on ADT, the controversial Anglo-American security and car auctions business run by Michael Ashcroft.

It was not clear from the 1991 acounts just how ADT treated security installations in the accounts. Competitors told me that it was common practice among their companies to bundle the cost of labour and other items in with the cost of the equipment when it was installed, to count that as an addition to the value of the installation (to capitalise it), and to treat it as an extra asset in the balance sheet. Some companies would then write off that cost over ten years, providing depreciation equal to 10pc of the capitalised cost each year. ADT, it appeared from the accounts, wrote some installations off over 14 or 15 years, thus knocking only perhaps 7pc off profits each year as depreciation, not the more widely used 10pc. That meant profits appeared higher.

But it also meant that when business was slack, as it was in 1991,and clients were going bust and abandoning security contracts, income from the installations stopped. No-one wants a second-hand alarm system. So while the equipment (and labour) had gone into the balance sheet as an asset, it had become effectively worth nothing when the contract was abandoned. And profits would have to bear the cost of depreciation for the remainder of the 14 or 15 years, though no income was coming in.

In reality, the whole question of accounting for alarm installations is vastly more complicated. ADT might well have found a different, sensible, answer. But it is easy to see how the fine print in the ADT accounts might prompt the sceptical investor to proceed with caution.

Do not despair if it all sounds desperately complicated. As you become more familiar with the game, you will find it easier to unravel. What should be clear, however, is that there are all sorts of questions lurking in the fine print, if you can root them out. And depreciation is certainly worth watching.

EXTRAORDINARY ITEMS

Notes to the accounts will also throw up any extraordinary items, such as unusual sales which have boosted profits, or heavy redundancy costs or write-offs which have held them back. There should be no great mystery about them, and most of the City will have taken them into account. Make a mental note of them when you assess the profits again. Sometimes it is possible to predict a big profit swing simply from the absence of one-off charges or credits in the coming year. The accounting regulators have swung the spotlight on to extraordinary items, and the way they are handled in accounts may be about to change, hopefully making it clear what is really going on. More about such things in the section on creative accounting.

SCRIP ISSUES

Once you have worked through the report and accounts, and struck up a nodding acquaintance with the contents, you are well on the way towards mastering an elementary crib on the coarse art of investment analysis. There are, however, a few more items which crop up fairly frequently, and repay attention. Scrip issues are generally the most welcome. The scrip issue comes under several different names – a capitalisation issue, a share bonus, or a free scrip issue. It is sometimes called a free scrip because no-one has to pay for the shares it doles out. Strictly speaking it is just a sophisticated piece of book-keeping. A company with a fistful of reserves transforms them into extra share capital, and gives the shares to the owners – the shareholders.

In reality, nothing is given away. All that happens is that the nominal capital increases, and everyone has more shares. The company itself is not, in theory, worth a penny more. So the share price should simply be adjusted to reflect the capital change. If there has been a one for one bonus, giving every shareholder twice the number of shares they had before, the price should halve. Nothing gained, nothing lost.

Psychologically, though, the impact is valuable. Shareholders love it. Time and again at annual meetings, it is the one thing shareholders care about; 'Please, Mr Chairman, could we have a scrip issue?' Good luck to them. News of a scrip issue usually sends shares up, and they may rise again just before the new shares are sent out, then again after they have been issued. It is an important sign of corporate confidence.

Take shares trading at 400p. On news of a one for one scrip, they might edge up to 405p. Ahead of the actual issue, they might touch 420p. After the issue, the price is halved to take account of the new shares. Then the price might pop up to 215p – equivalent to 430p before it all began. Wonderful what a little paper-shuffling can do.

Everyone likes to feel they are getting more for their money. It seems better to buy 500 shares at 200p each than 250 at 400p, or even 100 at £10 a time. When shares get too high, the market frowns. Anything over 400p is looking heavy, and heavy is not so much fun. There is a mass of investors who only buy 'penny' stocks – that is, shares selling at under £1 (a penny gets you nowhere these days). A scrip issue suits them. It cuts the price down to their size.

SHARE SPLITS

Sometimes companies achieve a similar effect by splitting their capital. Shares with a nominal value of £1 might be divided into two shares of 50p, or ten of 10p. Again, the reality is largely cosmetic. But it leaves the company looking more attractive, and that helps.

RIGHTS ISSUES

A rights issue is different. You have to pay for it. It involves selling new shares to existing shareholders. It is a means of raising cash, and giving all shareholders an equal chance to join in, if they wish.

In the late eighties and early nineties, rights issues have proved a distinctly mixed blessing. Most have been rescue efforts, pulling in desperately-needed cash to save the company from collapse. Weighed down by borrowings, companies have turned to shareholders to raise relatively cheap new money to pay off expensive loans. In many cases, shareholders have had cause to be thankful for small mercies. At least the company could manage a rights call. The very weakest simply went under because no-one was prepared to back a rights issue.

Some shareholders are unwilling, or unable, to put up extra money. So most companies arrange to have the issue underwritten. For a small commission, big investors agree to take up all of the new shares which other investors do not want. Normally, the new rights shares are sold about 20pc below the market price. If it falls below that while the issue is open, more shareholders will turn it down, and the underwriters have to step in and take the shares.

A few companies do it differently. They opt to sell the new shares way below the market, half price or less. This is called a deep discount rights. The shares appear cheap, and the company saves the cost of underwriting. Financially, it makes no great difference. In good times, it is a gesture of corporate confidence. In trickier times, the shares can slump way down towards the deep discounted level, and it all misfires.

When the market is reasonably calm, most rights issues are sweetened by forecasts of higher profits and dividends. That helps offset the depressing impact of more shares being thrown onto the market. If a rights flops, it can dog the shares for months, even years. Every time the price perks up, it will be hit by selling from underwriters seeking to get out.

Often rights issues are well left alone, particularly if they look like a rescue act by the old management. New management might be much better, though. Whatever, you lose little by refusing. You have the same number of shares as before, but since there will be more in issue, you just have a proportionately smaller slice of a larger cake.

If the terms of the issue are judged correctly, others will be willing to buy your rights. Calculating the premium can be complicated. Ask your broker or banker. It may be possible to sell part of your rights, and use the cash that raises to take up a small number of the new shares.

In reasonable markets, rights issues can generally be viewed as positive. What you really want is new shares from a smallish company under new management. It is a standard ploy for ambitious company promoters to buy into sleepy companies, then raise new capital by a heavy rights issue, giving themselves the opportunity to buy extra shares on the cheap.

Bigger companies can benefit too. The reputation and skills of the directors are what counts. The share price may take a while to settle down after a rights, but sometimes simply using the new money to pay off expensive loans can have a dramatic impact on profits. Or the money may be used to buy into exciting new ventures.

CLAWBACK

In recent years, rights have become less fashionable, replaced by a close cousin, the open offer and clawback. Companies sell new shares to a big investment house, or a group of investors, at a set price. The buying group agrees to allow shareholders to apply for (or claw back) some of those shares at the issue price, often in the same sort of proportion as would have ruled in a rights issue.

This method can mean the new shares are placed at a level closer to the market price than with a rights issue. It also has accounting advantages, allowing companies to treat goodwill in a way which does not reduce profits. Do not worry about that.

Clawback has been attacked as undermining the rights of small shareholders. The attack is well founded. If there are to be new shares in a company, then existing shareholders ought to get first chance at buying them. It is a way of increasing your share stake without incurring broking costs, and there is often a small profit in selling the rights. The swing to clawback marks yet one more small change, putting more profit into the pockets of big City bullies at the expense of the individual investor. The good clawback news for the company concerned is that it can be sure of getting the cash quickly, and can use it at short notice if a buying opportunity crops up. It also ensures instant City support for the scheme, and locks influential investors in more securely behind the management. It still leaves a nasty taste for those who think the shareholder – large or small – is the owner of the company, and should get whatever privileges are going.

CHAPTER FIVE
HOW DOES THE MARKET WORK?

Once you have a rough idea of what you are looking for, where do you find it? Nothing, of course, ever comes as simple as it might first seem. Buying shares on the Stock Exchange is not what it used to be. The Stock Exchange does not really exist any more, and many of the stockbrokers who are in business to buy and sell shares will not want to know about small-time individual investors.

The great grey tower block sitting in Throgmorton Street, slap in the centre of the City, close by the Bank of England and the Mansion House, is no longer where the action is. It might be called the Stock Exchange Tower, but now it houses only market officials and assorted stockbrokers. The trading floor has gone. The six-sided boxes which used to flash on TV screens so often have disappeared. No-one knows quite what to do with the space. Even the traded options market finally moved out on January 31, 1992. Share trading now takes place over the telephone, and over computer lines. You can glimpse the new dealing rooms, each owned by a different house, in the background whenever some City pundit comes on TV to tell you how the economy is going. There are vast halls, crammed with rows of desks, each desk bearing two or three screens, maybe more. The dealers, men and women, spend much of the day on one of three or four phones at their fingertips, while every so often a Tannoy system booms out an announcement or instruction.

Once upon a time, I used to be taken through a steel works, an engineering plant, or an automated bakery. I would feel sorry for the people who had to work there, day in, day out. Now I shudder every time I see the City's battery chickens cooped up at their desks, eyes fixed on the screens, ears abuzz with noise. Dreadful.

The old system was blown apart by Big Bang. In October 1986, 200 years of Stock Exchange history changed. It needed changes to ensure that London kept pace with international 24 hour trading. In the name of greater competition, Sir Gordon Borrie at the Office of Fair Trading forced the market to abandon the old idea of having brokers as one class of member to take orders to buy and sell from the public, and another class, the jobbers, to hold the shares, set the prices, and deal with the brokers.

For private investors. the old system was far superior. It was open to abuse, but escaped many of the conflicts of interest in the new system. Now jobbers and brokers can be combined into market-makers. Integrated investment houses are the City equivalent to one stop shopping. You can dream up a bid, employ the bankers to carry it through for you, and have their broking house make the market in your shares, and buy and sell the same shares for outside investors.

In theory, a 'Chinese Wall' stops one department telling the other what is going on. If the bank is working on a bid, it cannot tell the broking boys to pile into shares of the bid target. That would be illegal use of insider information. There are all sorts of measures to guard against it. Judge for yourself how well they work, and how many small, subtle, but enormously lucrative, advantages can be gained by doing the lot in-house. Believe me, you cannot begin to comprehend the fiddles, large and small, which go on – all within the rules, old chap, of course.

INSIDER TRADING

Insider trading – the use of privileged information – has existed as long as the stock market. Not so long ago – twenty or thirty years – everyone understood that a decent stockbroker was the one who got good information in good time. That was why you used him. A nod and a wink, part of the Old Pal's Act, ensured that the music went round and round, and everyone did quite nicely, thank you.

Share dealing was more exclusive then, of course. Now over twelve million people own shares, thanks largely to privatisation issues. But there was a great explosion of private investor interest in the eighties. Thousands of eager new investors rushed to buy and sell for themselves. Many did very well, too, until the Crash of October 1987. That wiped some out for ever. Many others are sitting tight, waiting for the real game to start again. It will. When it does, they will be joined by a new generation of investors. The next boom could be the most exciting yet, with more players than ever.

Be under no illusion, though. Insider trading takes place every day. It may be illegal, but it is impossible to stop, and extremely difficult to prove. The insider uses confidential information to buy or sell shares before the rest of the market knows what is going on. Every so often, someone is taken to court, and charged. Much more often, suspect cases are quietly dropped because the chances of winning a conviction are slim.

Most of those convicted are unsophisticated people playing for peanuts in a relatively naive way – amateur investors. The only big fish to get caught in this country was Geoffrey Collier, a top trader at merchant bank Morgan Grenfell. He got off with a relatively light sentence. They have been a shade tougher in America, sending ace arbitrageur Ivan Boesky to jail, along with banker Dennis Levine, and junk bond king Michael Milken. These highly publicised cases have been supported by a number of more modest convictions. But closer examination reveals that many of those convicted have later been let go. And the games go on.

In the City, there are syndicates of professionals making millions by swapping confidential information. The Stock Exchange monitors every unusual price rise. They happen almost every day. The Stock Exchange probably has a good idea of the identity of many of those involved. Proving it is a very different matter.

AGENTS AND PRINCIPALS

Big Bang has not made it any easier. Never mind the ethics of bundling sophisticated merchant banking together with private client broking. Think about it on a more mundane level. The broking firm which you may approach to buy shares for you as your agent could actually turn out to be a principal as well. Remember those terms – agent and principal – because they might crop up when you trade. Watch out for them.

The agent does what you tell him, and goes away and deals elsewhere for you. If he is a principal, he will buy or sell for you, but his firm may hold some of the shares you are trading in. His firm may actually sell you shares it is holding, or may actually buy your shares for itself. The broker should tell you this, and it should not influence your price. Sometimes it could get you a better deal. Just imagine, though, that your broker's firm has bought a large block of shares in a particular company. It got a good price because it bought so many. Every share it sells on may yield not just the normal commission, but a profit of 1p or 2p a share. Sometimes, individual salesmen/brokers are offered a piece of that profit if they hit selling targets. If you happen to ring, what are the chances that you might be steered towards the share in question? Make up your own mind.

That example – it happens – reflects a far greater conflict of interest than insider trading. Stretch it a shade further. Just suppose the broking house is also advising a particular company.

If that company wants to make a share issue – a clawback, perhaps, as mentioned earlier – it will be important to keep the shares up ahead of the deal, to ensure the company gets the best terms. Who is to say how many casual clients will be encouraged to buy in the days ahead of the deal? Later, when the broker has agreed to find buyers for the new shares, and the market is turning sticky, will the private clients be encouraged to take a few shares? Doing them a favour, letting them in on a good thing? Or stuffing them into something you cannot shift? Insider trading? Maybe. Maybe not. Anyone who plays the market must accept insider trading and conflicts of interest as facts of life. Few buy or sell shares without thinking they know better than the other person. For every buyer, someone is selling. It is the capitalist system in the raw. If it upsets you, keep out.

INVESTOR PROTECTION

After much huffing and puffing, the Government and the City have come up with new regulations designed to provide more investor protection than ever. You had not noticed? What with Barlow Clowes, dodgy insurance schemes, and bent investment brokers hitting the press? Oh dear.

The authorities have been trying – very trying, most of us in the business would say. Forests have been cleared to provide tons of paper to print the rules to be sent to thousands of people who cannot understand them, even if they want to. Hundreds of millions of pounds have been spent, trying to devise regulations to protect investors. They have achieved something – but less than the effort and expense might suggest.

The simple fact is that it is impossible to protect fools being parted from their money. And it is impossible to supervise a smooth salesperson all of the time. Sadly, all too many of us are a poor match for someone with a good, persistent line of patter.

The Financial Services Act covers all sorts of things financial. The share investor, though, needs to know about the Securities and Investments Board, 2, Bunhill Row, London, EC1Y 8RA (telephone 071 929 3652). This is meant to rule over a variety of lesser Self Regulating Organisations. The phone number gives you an advice line which will tell you if your investment adviser is authorised to do what he wants – especially whether he is allowed to take your money.

You can also check the status of advisers if you subscribe to Prestel on your TV. Call SIB for the information. Prestel is available at many public libraries, and your local Citizens Advice Bureau should also have the information.

Strictly speaking, SIB should not be your first call. Stockbrokers are covered by the Securities and Futures Authority, which runs a complaints bureau and an arbitration scheme for sums under £25,000. You can find that at The Stock Exchange Building, Old Broad Street, London, EC2N 1EQ (telephone 071 588 2355).

You might find you are dealing with an investment adviser who is covered better by FIMBRA, the Financial Intermediaries, Managers and Brokers Regulatory Association, at Hertsmere House, Marsh Wall, London, E14 9RW (telephone 081 538 8860).

Sadly, I cannot guarantee that any of the addresses or numbers are correct, or that you will find the right place to complain to with your first or second try. They all seem to move about, and change their names and responsibilities. Though I deal with them regularly, I still find myself getting shunted from one to another with irritating frequency. Keep at it, though, if you have a problem. You should get help in the end. And if you ring with a query, do explain to them just what it is someone is trying to sell you, or trying to get you to do. In some curious way, they cannot always be as helpful as they would wish. But they do find it useful to know what is going on. Even they recognise that the practice often differs from the theory they lay down.

If the worst comes to the worst, you might have to fall back on the Investors' Compensation Scheme. This covers you if your broker goes bust, or breaks the rules and loses you money. It could give you back the first £30,000 of any loss, and up to 90pc of the next £20,000. There are ombudsmen scattered around as a last resort.

Any sensible investor will be wary of committing more than £30,000 to any one firm. Even more clearly, the sensible investor avoids getting into a jam in the first place. Use your common sense, watch out for the angles, and you should be fine. Precious few of the sorry tales I come across involve people who have been as careful as they should have been. Usually – not always – the victims have contributed to their own downfall. Follow the rules in this book, and you should avoid that.

WHERE TO BUY

Alerted yet undaunted by this alarmist stuff, where do you actually turn to get on with the business of share buying? There are four main channels; a member of the Stock Exchange; a bank or building society; a telephone execution-only service; or a dealer in securities belonging to FIMBRA. Some of these may be dressed up as share shops, though when last I looked, most seemed to have done a bunk or given up the ghost.

STOCKBROKERS

Despite my grim warnings, stockbrokers – members of the Stock Exchange – are still much your best bet. Their conduct is covered by the rules of the Stock Exchange, and strictly covered. If they should go bust (or get 'hammered' in Stock Exchange terms), or you can prove that they have cost you money by breaking the rules, then you will qualify for the Investors' Compensation Scheme. Or you could win an award from the SFA arbitration scheme. It might be better still by the time you read this. Many brokers are convinced that they should return to the old Stock Exchange system of unlimited compensation, and are trying to restore such a plan. Quite right.

The motto of the Stock Exchange is 'My Word Is My Bond', and it still means something. Most stockbrokers are honourable, and will handle your orders carefully and correctly. Their investment advice requires greater caution. Most give honest, well-meaning advice. But the small investor cannot reasonably expect to take up too much of the time, or attention, of the most skilled and experienced brokers.

Different services are developing. Some brokers offer a no-frills, discount dealing service. They simply do what you tell them, buying or selling on your instructions, charging a commission, and giving no advice. Others will manage your money, send regular portfolio valuations and such, and allow you access to research ideas. This may be too costly for the small investor. In the middle, there are firms offering a little advice, perhaps some cheap dealing in certain circumstances, with extra charges for additional facilities.

As a rule, you will find it cheaper to deal with one of the brokers outside London. Lower overheads allow them to charge less, and they often have more time for individual investors.

Many provincial brokers make a real effort to cultivate the small player, seeking to build a relationship which they hope will pay off over time. They need the business more than the London broker, and make that extra effort. There is the added advantage that it may be possible to pop into the office to see them. Face to face discussions are much better than dealing on the phone all of the time.

So do not spurn the local man. He may not be quite in touch with the City gossip, but he may compensate with a sounder knowledge of local companies, and smaller situations. For the private investor, that can be invaluable, especially in the early stages of a bull market. Spotting promising smaller companies before London wakes up can be enormously rewarding.

One note of caution. Make sure that the local broker (or, indeed, any broker) is what he says he is. Check that the firm does belong to the Stock Exchange. DO NOT TAKE IT ON TRUST. It should be a mere formality, of course. But sometimes small share shops, or local dealers of some sort spring up. They create the impression of being proper brokers, and rely on no-one bothering to check. They can do the most diabolical things.

There is one other distinction to keep in mind. We touched on it earlier. Always check whether your broker is acting as agent or principal when he trades for you. Just make sure you watch for the angle behind his advice.

Many brokers these days will try to talk you out of going directly into shares. They do not want the trouble and expense of dealing in small quantities. It costs them as much to process your £1,000 deal as it does to handle one worth £50,000 – though they will certainly be charging the big trader less than the full rate of commission. Such brokers will nudge you towards a unit trust. They may have one of their own. Forget it. If you are reading this book, you want to do it yourself.

Many big London brokers will turn up their noses at anything under £100,000. Fair enough. They are not the sort of people you want anyway. They will not spare you the time and trouble you deserve. Do not get indignant at being turned away. For a successful investment relationship to work, both sides need to be interested.

Actually finding a suitable broker is not easy. Ideally, you want someone you can talk to as an equal, someone you can eventually trust and confide in, who can spare a minute or two when you need it. Personal recommendation is best, but you can only really judge by working with someone. If things do not click, go elsewhere. IT IS YOUR MONEY AT STAKE. No matter how superior they might seem, brokers are a cross between order clerks and bookmakers – they take the bets and pay the winners. You pay the piper, make sure you call the tune. Watch the financial press for advertisements. Then ask anyone you think might know about the firm of your choice. A big name may not be enough. Some of the big boys are super, but you may well not be important enough to matter to them. You could find yourself left with some fresh-faced graduate, learning the business. He may mean well, but he may not manage too well.

The Stock Exchange is helpful. Write and ask for a list of brokers willing to take on smaller clients. The Exchange keeps such a list, regularly updated, and will be happy to send it. While you are about it, ask the Exchange for their other booklets for new investors. They are excellent.

THE BANK

If you cannot find a suitable broker, it is worth going to your bank. No matter what the TV advertisements suggest, the banks are not really that well geared up to handle individual investors. But they are working on it.

They have improved enormously, and most now own stockbroking firms, or have strong links with them. They have a recognised, clearly defined system for handling new clients. Some branches will be more useful than others.

Charges vary. Special cheap rates for privatisations can be misleading, and some charges do look on the heavy side. The banks will be able to put you on to more sophisticated broking operations, with some access to research, if you wish. Try it and see. It is hard to give more practical advice. So far, I have seen too little of the results to judge.

THE BUILDING SOCIETY

Share dealing at building societies has been gaining ground as a result of the privatisation issues. Some societies offer a fairly full service, and actually own a stockbroker. Others have close links. Like the banks, any service is likely to be second best by comparison with direct contact with a broker. But it may suit you. At least with the banks and building societies, you are dealing with trustworthy organisations. There may be mistakes, but not dishonesty.

TELEPHONE SERVICES

Dealers who operate a phone-in service, concentrating on execution only, without offering advice, are springing up. Led by ShareLink, which is controlled by British Telecom, these can serve a useful purpose for small investors who know what they are doing. They offer relatively keenly priced and efficient trading. Check first that they are proper members of some regulated authority, and look carefully at the wording of any contract they send you. While it seems unfair to suggest it, be careful about newly established operators. At least one went under because it could not cope with the demand generated by one of the privatisations. There was no dishonesty, just a muddle.

INVESTMENT ADVISERS AND SHARE SHOPS

There are still a few investment advisers who are not quite stockbrokers, but who appear much the same from the outside. Some are dressed up as share shops. These will take your orders, give you advice, and charge what appear to be normal rates of commission. They will be governed by FIMBRA, and will often be staffed by former stockbrokers. In fact, they will be passing your orders on to a stockbroker, and sharing commission with them.

In many cases, they will be keen to recommend shares and to get you to buy them. These are the successors to the old licensed dealers in securities, the kind of people who used to operate what was the Over-The-Counter market. That used to deal in shares not listed on the London Stock Exchange. It led to a succession of duds, and proved extremely costly to thousands of small investors who got caught up in it through the likes of Harvard Securities or Ravendale.

Such firms should be avoided. They almost always act as principals. That means they are selling you shares they own. Almost invariably, they will have bought a large block at well below the normal market price. They will then try to sell them to you at the market price, or perhaps offer you the chance of buying a little below the quoted price. Sometimes, they may have gone into the market themselves to buy a few shares, and tickle the listed price still higher before they come to you. Either way, they will be taking an enormous turn between the price they have paid, and the price you pay.

The idea will not be to do you a favour and make you a profit – it is amazing how many people still believe such nonsense – but to shunt stock through at a profit to them. Early in 1992, I began hearing stories of one firm which was buying millions of shares in one small, unspectacular UK company, and selling them on to clients at 1½p each. The proper market price was 1p to buy at first – then dropped to ¾p. So the dealers were doubling their money.

The wilder ones will try to sell you shares in companies which do not have a proper Stock Exchange listing here. Usually these companies will be quoted on some regional American exchange. Usually the promoter will have bought a massive number of them at a fraction of a penny, and be selling them in the UK at many times the original price – I have heard of some sold at 50 times cost. Usually, it will be impossible to sell them in America, or anywhere else. Sometimes the stock will carry perfectly legal restrictions which forbid it being sold in America for a certain time – that it why it is being knocked out in this country. You will not be told that. The only buyer will be the smooth talker who sold them to you. And he will rarely be anxious to take them back. Now and then, the shares will be in companies which do not exist.

It may sound improbable. Investment advisers everywhere will assure you no such thing ever happens in any firm they have been with. At the risk of being unfair to a few legitimate operators, I suggest steering clear of any such advisers. The regulators rarely keep up with what is going on, and perfectly respectable firms can change character overnight if some villain buys in. It happens.

In the old days, I used to think there could be a place for some of these independent investment advice cum broking firms, offering a higher-risk, sales-based service to those prepared to take a bit of a gamble. Sadly, I now think I was wrong to give them the benefit of the doubt. In the end, far too many proved bent, or simply turned bent when the pressure came on.

The salesman often use the same old, well-rehearsed pitch to appeal to you. If, for example, they plead that they are doing you a favour, ensuring you have a winner first time out, because they want you as a regular customer, slam down the phone. You are being fed the good old sucker line.

WHAT IT COSTS

Share dealing costs have been thrown into confusion since Big Bang abolished fixed commissions. Anything goes now. Inevitably, it goes higher and higher.

It would be foolish to be too dogmatic about what you ought to pay. Levels of service vary so much, and costs are rising all of the time. Instead of cutting charges to generate more business when there is little going on, the investment community prefers to bump them up, every time. In central London and the bigger provincial cities, too many are trapped paying silly rents for fancy properties. While rents may be plummeting all around them, they are committed to paying dearly for leases they took out in more prosperous time. So they think they have to charge fat fees.

At the time of writing, it seems that between £15 and £20 is a fair figure for a cut-price, execution-only deal. Other firms charge a minimum of £35 a deal, maybe more. Do not be misled by the privatisation offers. They are too low to last.

Do not be tempted into believing that the cheapest may be as good as the best. It may suit you, but some are are tempted into dealing with dubious firms to try to save £5 or £10 on dealing costs. It is not worth it. Any share transaction will involve quite a significant amount of your money. It is not worth jeopardising it for the sake of a few pounds. The most unexpected things happen from time to time. Even if a cut-price merchant is playing straight, but simply gets in a muddle, you will rue the day you got involved. It could take months before things are unscrambled, and you get your money or your shares.

It may also be a false economy dealing cheap unless you are getting a proper price for your shares. A difference of 1p when you are selling 1,000 shares is worth £10. Will the house offering the cheapest dealing cost get you the best price? Perhaps. Perhaps not. Rather than trade with those who reduce dealing charges by holding your order, lumping it in with others in one big deal to save costs, it may be better to settle for a firm price at the time you trade.

A good broker will take time and trouble to ensure that you do get the best price on offer. Some banks, for example, deal with the market-maker they own. If he is not offering the finest price, you miss out. Paying a little over the odds on commission may sometimes be cheapest in the end. This year, next year, some time, the Stock Exchange plans to introduce an automatic dealing system. At one stage, it was supposed to reduce costs for the private investor. I doubt it . . . if it comes, when it comes.

ACCOUNT TRADING

The Stock Exchange trading calendar is divided into periods called accounts. These are normally two weeks long, three weeks around bank holidays. Most accounts end on a Friday. All bills are settled on the Monday ten days later. If you buy a share and sell it within the account, you pay only one commission to your broker. So short-term, in and out dealing costs less.

It also opens the magic opportunity of making a profit without actually laying down any cash. If you buy and sell in the same account at a profit, your broker simply sends you a cheque for the difference. Buy, and sell at a loss, and you send him a cheque.

Account trading is very risky. You need a volatile share price, good judgement, and fine timing. You not only have to make enough to cover dealing cost, but also to cover the spread between the market-maker's buying and selling price. Most newspapers quote the middle price of a share. When you actually deal, you discover the difference. The market-maker will buy, say, Marks & Spencer at 290p, and sell at 294p. The price in the paper will be 292p, the middle price.

It might appear that if the shares rise to 297p, you are making a nice profit. Not so. When the middle was 292p, you would have paid 294p for your Marks & Sparks. With 297p the middle price, the market-maker would be quoting 295p to 299p. When you sell, you would get 295p, a profit of just 1p. That, though, is before dealing costs. In practice, you would need at least 297p to break even, after costs. So to make a profit, you would need Marks & Sparks to advance to 299p middle price, a rise of 7p.

Trading in the account is much tougher than it first appears. It is not sensible unless you have lots of spare cash, an iron nerve, and instant access to a broker who will trade quickly and shrewdly for you. You will need to trust each other also. He will understand that the chances of you making a loss are high, and you may need to rely on him to deal for you sometimes before he can tell you what he is doing, if he feels it is in your interest when prices start to change quickly.

The odds are also loaded against you because the market-makers have a pretty shrewd idea which shares attract account traders. They know the traders will be looking to sell towards the end of an account, on the Thursday afternoon or Friday. So they tend to shift prices down a notch in anticipation, eating away more of any potential profit.

Banish dreams of account trading until you are confident you understand it well. Then, perhaps, you will decide it is too risky for you. It does help to demonstrate, however, how the costs of dealing can mount up.

The account system is another time-honoured tradition which may be for the chop. The Stock Exchange wants to do away with it, partly because it does not conform with other systems around the world, and may upset our new Common Market masters. The big investors are not too keen on it. Many of them do not use the system. They pay when the shares they buy are actually delivered. Once again, the balance is likely to be tilted a little more away from the small investor.

SHARE LISTINGS

Not every share on the London Stock Exchange is equal in the eyes of the Exchange. Some shares have a full listing, while others are quoted on the Unlisted Securities Market. There used to be a Third Market for fledgling companies, but that has been abolished.

Generally speaking, shares with a full listing are the biggest, safest, and most solid companies – though in the early nineties, precious few companies looked absolutely safe. To earn a full listing, they must show a three year trading record, and must offer at least 25pc of their capital for sale on flotation. USM companies need a two year trading record.

In practice, the differences are scarcely worth bothering about. Some fully-listed companies are clapped-out shadows, clinging on to a share quote, and far more risky than any USM stock. So listing distinctions are not too good a guide. What matters more is liquidity – whether it is easy to deal in reasonable quantities at reasonable prices. Some USM companies are more liquid than fully listed ones.

RULE 535

This is a special Stock Exchange rule which permits limited dealings in the shares of smaller, more obscure companies. Effectively it is a matched market, which means that the market-maker marries willing buyers with willing sellers. He keeps lists of both. Obviously this is not too good, and until you really understand what is going on, is not for you. Some ghost companies linger on in this form, companies which once had some better listing, and have slipped into obscurity. And there are sometimes promising new, but small, companies.

BUSINESS EXPANSION SCHEMES

Some shares traded under rule 535 are in companies covered by the Business Expansion Scheme. Shares in BES companies can be floated under strict rules which allow the cost of the investment to be set off against tax. The shares then have to be held for at least five years to keep the tax concession, which is granted only to the original purchasers.

Sometimes BES investors need to sell before the five years is up, and the shares find their way into rule 535 dealings. Be careful. Because they are being sold without the tax concession, they are not worth nearly as much to a second buyer. And it could be extremely difficult to resell them. Sadly, many BES issues have proved to be poor investments, even with the tax saving. The small companies they promoted have been hit hard by the recession.

CHAPTER SIX
PICKING PENNIES OFF A PLATE

Oh happy days. Lights, action, movement, sound-track of Gladys Knight singing 'The Way We Were', and the camera pans across the street. Memories.

It is 7.30 on a chill winter morning. Queues are forming outside a grey City bank. The office juniors are there, each with a thick wad of papers under the arm. Old ladies with plastic bags bulging chat to porters from the meat market. The odd old-style City gent, velvet collar and brolly, reads his *Financial Times* alongside men in long black coats and beards, guarding crammed cardboard boxes beside them on the pavement. A few people are frantically scribbling on forms, writing cheques. Secretaries join the line as police shepherd it away from the edge of the pavement, and the press cameras click.

By 10 o'clock, with the bank doors long open, the queue has become a scrum, with sheaves of paper being shuffled from hand to hand, and sleek City brokers directing office boys as they push through the crowd, throwing bundles across the counter into wicker baskets. At one minute past ten, the bank cries 'Time', cashiers slam down the barriers across the counter, and commissionaires move to close the doors.

That was how it used to be. Another successful new issue would be on its way, application lists closed at 10.01a.m., heavily oversubscribed. As the eighties gave way to the nineties, the picture changed. The queues grew shorter, and when the doors were closed, it would be some minor Government minister milking the TV cameras, anxious to gain political capital from the latest privatisation issue.

When times are hard, the flow of new issues dries up. There are opportunities to make money, but they are offered to selected clients only. It is left to the big money state sell-offs to provide some excitement. And though there have been a few disappointments – the Scottish power issues especially – most have been well worth backing.

Never fear. There will be a return to the time-honoured City game of stagging – buying shares in a new issue, hoping to sell at a handsome profit as soon as dealings begin. In the mid-eighties, hundreds of millions of pounds, much of it borrowed money, would pour in chasing almost any new issue. It was routine for offers to attract ten times the amount of cash they were seeking. Now and then, the odd issue would be 100 times over-subscribed. It was as close as most of us can get to money for nothing. The chance will come again, be sure.

STAGGING

Outsiders may sneer, but there is nothing wrong with stagging. It provides a little extra excitement and helps make the share game such fun. From the modest punter who puts up £200 hoping to make a quick £20 or more to the syndicate which might apply for £100m of shares, it is a gambling bonanza which leaves Las Vegas standing, and bookmakers limping way down the field. One burly City broker counted his stagging profits in tens of millions in 1985. Dozens of groups of fund managers, bankers, brokers, and boys about the City worked together more discreetly to make tidy fortunes. In a matter of minutes when dealings started, they would scoop more profit than the average British company could earn in a year of hard slog.

No need to moralise. No matter how the notion of get rich quick spivvery may upset you, while the system lasts, there is little point in not taking your share. Strip away the pious nonsense about creating a share-owning democracy, and you see that a Tory Government has cynically exploited the new issue market to create privatisation profits for people in a fashion most likely to encourage them to vote Conservative. Freeing major industries from state control may have helped improve their efficiency. But in too many cases it has meant short term profits for those who buy shares, and higher bills from near-monopoly enterprises, bearing down on poorer people who could not afford to join the share game. Pretty close to robbing the poor to pay the fairly rich.

The system is constructed to favour the stag, to yield quick profits to those who support new share issues. The message really came home to the masses in the autumn of 1984 with the British Telecom flotation. All you had to do was fill in a form, write a cheque, take it to the bank or post it, and sit back and wait for the profits to pour in. For every pound you put up, there was a profit of 86p on the first day of dealing. A couple of months later, there was a profit of 140p for every 100p. Oh, the joys of the capitalist class.

It was not just privatisation issues which yielded fabulous profits. There was Laura Ashley, the home furnishing and fashion group which has since fallen on harder times. When it floated, it was easy to believe it was a good thing. The shops were booming all over Britain and France, with plans to conquer America. No political meddling, just a good commercial company, floating shares to help the founding family take some cash out and to give the company more for future growth. Every share you bought at 135p could have been sold at 185p on the first day of dealing.

An exception? Not at all. In 1986 and 1987, new issues galore roared to a handsome profit in first-time dealings. One or two had their sticky moments, but anyone who stagged the major issues made a killing. Even the notoriously risk-prone British Airways lifted off to a thrilling flight.

You will have noticed that the examples come from the mid-eighties, or earlier. The game almost ended with the October '87 Crash, except for privatisations. But stories of old glory are worth telling. I cannot guarantee the timing. But the happy days will return. Read this chapter, note the contents, and be prepared to make the most of them when they do.

Something for nothing hardly sounds like the way the City normally works. But the real operators know they are giving a little something to the masses in return for a much bigger take for themselves. And so long as the stock market is in fair to average form, making money on new issues is like picking pennies off a plate. The only problem is elbowing aside all of the others scrambling for the pickings.

Once people realise that they are on offer again, the pickings could be fatter than ever before. Millions of people began to get the hang of it in the eighties. In the nineties, there will be many more eager to join in at the right time. The more money involved, the bigger the profits – so long as you know what you are doing.

Because the new issue system is geared to success, your friendly issuing house needs you, big punter or small, when the action starts. A good issue is one which gives something to everyone, leaving them all feeling happy. No broker or banker worth his salt tries to squeeze the last penny out of a new issue. If a company starts stock market life at a discount, a cloud could hang over it for years. Expansion plans are inhibited, goodwill is gone. If you lose money backing a new issue, the sponsors have got it wrong, not you. NEW ISSUES ARE DESIGNED TO GIVE YOU A PROFIT.

THE IDEAL WAY INTO SHARES

For those new to share trading, subscribing for a new issue is the ideal way into the stock market. You pay no commission to stockbrokers, no VAT, no stamp duty, and there is no market-maker taking a middleman's turn. No hidden extras need worry you. The price you pay is the price on the application form. You can skip the broker, bank or investment dealer. Simply cut the coupon out of your newspaper, and post it with a cheque. Often there are special low-price dealing services advertised with the big issues, and selling can be as simple as lifting a telephone, or popping into your bank or building society. Easy.

OFFERS FOR SALE

Most big new issues are carried out through a straightforward offer for sale. This will be arranged (or sponsored) by the issuing house, usually a merchant bank or a stockbroker. News of it will appear on most City pages. The best general early warning system is in the *Investors Chronicle*, or specialist new issue tipping sheets. *The Mail On Sunday* also prints a crude new issue alert.

Full details come in a prospectus, which has to be published in at least two national newspapers. Almost all prospectuses appear in the *Financial Times*. They are also available from the issuing house, and sometimes from the banks.

A prospectus can run to 120 pages – more in some privatisations. The real block-busters are not normally on offer to individual investors. In their place, there are mini-prospectuses, which still run to 20 pages or more.

A full prospectus can be a daunting document. It is hard to believe anyone, even broking backroom boys, reads the whole of some of the full privatisation documents. Even ploughing right through a normal prospectus could leave you with a nasty headache, an impressive growth of beard, and very little idea of what is going on. Do not be put off. The theory is that everyone should be encouraged to read all about shares before they buy. The theory is sound enough. In practice, the sheer bulk and complexity of most prospectuses is enough to scare most people off for life. Do not worry. A full prospectus is an optional extra for all but the really serious, big money investors – or those with experience enough to light on the pages where they know they need to look.

A few issues publish a mini-prospectus in the press. Often this is little more than an application form bearing the company's name. It usually gives no details of the company's business or profits. It is handy to have the application form more freely available, but this trend has been going too far. Do not consider making a serious decision from a mini-prospectus unless you have discovered what the company is about from somewhere else.

WHAT YOU NEED TO KNOW

All you really need to know is what the City thinks of the shares. If the boys in the market do not fancy them, they do not have a chance, no matter what you think. It is no good being the lone genius who spots the potential in a new issue. Success or failure will be determined by the weight of money sent in. If that is low, the issue will flop, no matter how brilliant the company. This is one instance where it is no use at all being a contrary thinker. If you are right, and everyone else wrong, wait to buy the shares at a discount, after dealings begin and the issue has flopped.

Finding out what the crowd thinks can be as easy as asking your broker, reading the City pages (you will soon learn who gets it right most often), or watching the grey market, if there is one. None of these is infallible, but until you get pretty smart, they will do better than you on your own. Your broker might frown, but the grey market dealers might be the best guide of all. Officialdom does not approve, and most have been driven out. The grey market operates outside the Stock Exchange, with traders offering to buy and sell new issues before official dealings begin. It is almost a form of betting, and in the early nineties, City betting house IG Index was the only grey market operator left plugging on through the recession. IG Index provides a genuine betting service. and though the IG prices are normally a good indicator, they are not always right. Well worth checking, though.

If any of the unofficial guides – brokers, press, or grey market – is uncertain about an issue, opt out. Your chances of scoring as a stag will be slim. Do not be tempted. Ask yourself how you have been so smart as to spot something good that the experts have missed. And then ask yourself if you need your head examining.

READING THE PROSPECTUS

A glance at the prospectus will tell you who is selling how many shares for what price. There will be pages about the history and present state of the company, but little about the future. That is a shame, but the Stock Exchange imposes strict rules on profit forecasts and such to stop dubious promoters projecting an unrealistically rosy glow over what lies ahead. That makes sense.

There will be a profit record, perhaps a profit forecast, and a dividend forecast. And there will be a calculation of the price earnings ratio, and the dividend yield, two basic statistics to compare with other quoted companies in the same line of business. That gives an easy, worthwhile guide to roughly what the share price should be. Watch out. Do not get trapped into comparing the prospective – future – earnings ratio and dividend yield with the historic – past – pe ratio and yield on other companies. It is easy to get a flattering impression of a new issue that way.

Deeper in the document will be words from the chairman on why the company is being floated. The more cash being raised for expansion, the better. Find out whether the board are simply lining their own pockets by selling lots of shares. Feel more confident if the continuing directors are keeping a sizeable stake, but not a majority of the shares. That way, they will be committed to working for themselves and other shareholders, but will lack the power to shoo away any would-be bidder without consulting shareholders. Big shareholders should also give some undertaking that they will hold the shares for at least a year, maybe more. You do not want them dumping a lot of stock just after you have bought in.

Check, too, how much pay is linked to profits. That helps, in small doses. Share incentives are also good, though they should not be over-generous. Around 5pc of the capital ear-marked to reward directors for good performance is reasonable, with another 5pc or so for employees. Frown at anything more. It may help get profits and perhaps the share price moving over the short term, but could be an incentive to use accounting methods which inflate published profits. That can back-fire.

How well I recall the long discussions with an earnest Sir Ralph Halpern when he was still chairman of Burton Group. In his £1m plus pay years, he would lecture on the importance of incentives. I was cursed for attacking a scheme which would have given the Burton board millions of pounds in potentially lucrative share options. When it all went wrong, the old board was desperately keen to deny that the rush into property development had been inspired by a need to keep profits coming through to generate the performance which kept cash pouring into board pay. Yet the ill-timed dash into property cost Burton hundreds of millions of pounds in losses, and almost brought the company to its knees. If it had worked, it would have supported earnings just as the shopping boom slowed. And kept board pay booming.

Watch the profit record. Check the notes to see there are no extraordinary or exceptional items which distort the profits in one year. Iron them out, if they do, to try to establish how smooth the course of normal trading runs. Look for unusually high interest payments, or rising interest charges. That might indicate how badly the company needs new money – and the scope for growth if the new cash can eliminate borrowings, cut interest charges and allow more profits through to new shareholders.

In smaller issues, or newer companies, be especially careful to check changes in capital. These can be difficult to unravel. Sometimes you will be astonished and dismayed to see how little the directors paid for their shares, particularly when they have recently sold a business in to form the company being floated. Every so often, I come across a venture where the promoters end up with the majority of the shares in return for a fledgling company whose value depends largely on hope. Actual profits or real assets will be thin on the ground. Or some directors who paid 1p for shares being sold at 40p. No matter how tempting the prospects, walk away.

NAMES TO WATCH

'Who's who' can be very important in determining how an issue will go. Check the sponsors – the merchant bank or broker behind the issue. Even the City's finest make mistakes, and get greedy or over-confident, and over-price an issue. But sponsorship by one of the better-known, quality names can be worth a great deal. The league table changes frequently, so ask your broker about the current state of play. Sometimes someone hits a hot streak – or goes stone cold. And success tends to attract the better prospects, the good companies looking to float. Morgan Grenfell was the superstar in the mid-eighties, but got caught in Guinness scandal and ended in a terrible mess.

In the first rank of merchant banks,, Warburg, Barings, Kleinwort Benson, Rothschild, Schroder Wagg, Lazard Brothers, Robert Fleming and County Natwest all have their strengths. Charterhouse, Hambros, and Barclays Merchant Bank have their moments, but Samuel Montagu will take a long while to recover from sponsoring the flotation of Robert Maxwell's Mirror Group Newspapers. Singer & Friedlander and Brown Shipley rank as also-rans, with Henry Ansbacher handicapped by old Maxwell links, and Guinness Mahon damned by the dismal failure of their miserable Business Expansion Scheme efforts.

Top of the broking heap is Cazenove, a firm of legendary placing power. If they push an issue, the boys will back it. They have to, if they want to stay in the club when the real goodies are passed around. Rowe & Pitman, now part of Warburg, is up there as well. James Capel consistently ranks high, but the ubiquitous UBS Phillips & Drew suffers from Blue Arrow links and from being too close to many troubled property companies.

Personal prejudice prompts me to sound a note of caution about the American-controlled invaders. They have enormous financial muscle, and some have great skill. On the whole, their methods still appear more aggressive than those employed by the better British houses, and their pricing tends to leave less for the individual investor. Goldman Sachs is widely admired, but as an issuing house, it must suffer from being very closely associated with support for Maxwell in the later period when he was behaving in truly disgraceful fashion.

DANGER ZONE

It is harder to be specific about other houses to avoid. Some small brokers are outrageous. How they survive in this supposedly tightly regulated era merely demonstrates that, no matter how tough the rules might appear, they do not always work too well. Other small brokers are excellent. But names, owners, and personalities are apt to change so fast that it would be unwise to try to list them. Some of the most interesting ones will be newly-formed houses, led by characters who have decided to break away from the big names.

Sadly, it would be remiss not to point out that the bigger, sounder companies generally gravitate towards the bigger, sounder houses when they seek flotation. Smaller issuing houses almost invariably have to compete for the less attractive propositions.

Take special care over American companies which float in London instead of their own country. They usually plead it is cheaper and quicker here. Almost – almost – invariably they have turned out to be duds.

FORM-FILLING TACTICS

The way you fill in the application form can be vital. Do read the instructions carefully, and do sign your cheque. More applications are rejected because of unsigned cheques than anything. If it says cross the cheque, cross it. If it asks for applications in units of 100 shares, do not ask for 150. Do not try to be clever. The system can only cope with simplified procedures. The issuing bank cannot spare the time and trouble to handle variations. It throws them out.

Look carefully at the cut-off points. Try to pitch your application just above them. For example, where applications should be for units of 200 shares up to 1,000 shares, then for units of 500 up to 5,000 shares, and finally for units of 1,000 shares thereafter, it makes sense to go for 1,500 shares, or for 6,000 if you have the money. The sponsors have formed natural breaks at 1,000 and 5,000 shares. They may use them when it comes to scaling down applications. So shoot high.

Anyone applying for up to 1,000 shares might get, say, 300. Those asking for between 1,100 and 5,000 might get 800, and people over 5,000 might get 40pc of what they sought. By going for a slot just above the natural break (most people will gravitate towards those breaks), you might shift yourself into a higher allotment. So, in the example, anyone asking for 6,000 shares might get 2.400, whereas applications for 5,000 might get only 800. Sometimes that little extra step can pay off with a disproportionately large allotment. The example may overstate the advantages, but the theory is sound. Any extra edge is worth having when you are chasing a winner.

And please, please, please, pay attention to the closing date and time. Application lists almost always close at one minute past ten in the morning, rarely staying open longer, and then only if the issue flops. If you miss the post, or cannot reach the receiving bank on time, that is it. No amount of pleading, no sob stories, will get you in. Miss the close, and you have had it. Most privatisations allow you to hand forms in at a local bank up to the day before. That is a safe, sensible way of doing it.

A really successful launch can be oversubscribed 100 times, with £1.1bn chasing £10m worth of shares, so the odds are against you. Every application will be scaled down, and it is up to the issuing house to choose how this is done. The bigger the demand, the smaller the chances of getting what you ask for – but the fatter the opening premium when dealing starts. What you lose on the swings, you may gain on the roundabout.

Some companies – especially privatisations – deliberately favour small investors. This happens, too, with some of the bigger, nationally known names when they come to market. They buy a little goodwill by spreading shares around. Smaller, more specialist operators may prefer fewer, larger shareholders. They will cost less to service. Watch the press for clues.

The more shares you ask for, the more you are likely to get – except when there is a pretty clear warning that those trying to be too greedy will get nothing at all. Some heavily subscribed privatisations have chopped jumbo applications off without a single share. The rough rule of thumb is that if over-subscription might mean scaling down heavily, it is easier to give nothing at all to those who would only have got a tenth or less of what they sought. But there is no easy advance guidance. Use your common sense.

Many heavily subscribed issues hold a ballot to decide which applications get shares. The ballot may be weighted to favour bigger applications, so while a cheque for £2,000 may win no more shares than a lucky one for £200, the £2,000 cheque may be ten times more likely to get something than the £200 one.

USE YOUR PARTNER

Your partner – husband or wife – can be a vital investment aid. Never make one application where two will legally do. Be sensible, though. Since Keith Best MP was prosecuted for making multiple applications in the British Telecom issue, the game has changed. Check the fine print. Privatisations clearly state that it is illegal to make multiple applications. A lot of computer time and effort is now devoted to highly sophisticated methods of tracking down multiples. That days are gone when your goldfish or your cat could make a killing in the new issue market.

Privatisations have made it clear that applications must only be for the benefit of the applicant. You should not persuade others to apply for you, in return for a share of their profits.

You certainly cannot put in on behalf of other people without telling them. You can, however, apply on behalf of your children under 18. Study the forms for details of what you should do. In state sell-offs where there are advantages to be gained from prior registration, make sure you register the children in advance as well.

There is no blanket ban against multiple applications. Strictly speaking, it is frowned upon. But many issuing houses are quite happy to see it happen. It makes any issue appear more successful. Unless it is spelt out, multiples are not illegal. The worst that can happen is that your forms will be thrown out. Some houses will turn a blind eye, especially if an issue is not doing too brilliantly.

Making multiple applications, backed by enormous bank overdrafts, used to be a cottage industry. Professional punters employed a small army of pensioners to write cheques, fill forms, and address envelopes by the thousand. Cats and goldfish galore crept in. Even now, when the stags are running, City litterbins are stuffed with discarded prospectuses, each with the application form missing. Litter levels can be a simple clue to the likely success of an issue. So can newspaper sales counters. Sometimes punters pull up at the printing works with small vans to carry off thousands of copies of editions which bear the application forms. You must have the real thing. Photocopies are not accepted.

BULLYING THE BANK MANAGER

Bullying bank managers to get them to extend sufficiently large overdrafts is also important in successful stagging. Managers know you must put up more money than you will actually be required to pay out in a big share issue. Normally, only cheques attached to successful applications are cashed – though that does vary. Because applications in a winner will be scaled down, a cheque for any surplus is sent back immediately the allotments are announced. Much of the loan is only needed for a few days. Then the real stag will be selling quickly, and running to bank his pay-out cheque as soon as possible.

The risks for any bank are small, so long as you are being sensible. Officially, bank managers are not too sure about stagging. But they can be persuaded. Ask for a stagging facility. The manager will charge you a hefty arrangement fee, so he gets his share. If you earn enough –

usually over £20,000 – take out a bank gold card. They usually allow you an overdraft of up to £10,000 at preferential rates, without prior consultation. Threaten to take your account elsewhere, to get a gold card from another bank, if your man is too difficult. After all, he needs your custom.

TRAPS FOR THE UNWARY

All of this may sound marvellous fun, a magic way of making money. But there are traps for the unwary, the reckless, and the feckless. New issues do flop sometimes. If you get it wrong, you could end up with many more shares than you really want, or can afford, in an issue which is going to open at a discount. There is no way out, should that happen. You cannot simply cancel your cheque if the issue looks like going bad. Once you have sent your application, you are on the hook. You can be prosecuted for cancelling your cheque.

That explains why there are queues on the morning a good issue closes. Some people have too much cash riding on it to leave anything to chance. Post your application form too far in advance, and you run the risk of a late change in the market mood. A promising issue could be left out in the cold, and your would-be winner could turn sour, after your cheque is in. The man in the last-minute queue has done all he can to avoid getting caught out. Even he has no guarantee. There can be up to ten days between applications closing and share dealings opening, though it is usually less. Always check the timing before you play.

And do not go absolutely mad. The surest-looking thing can go wrong. When you decide what to go for, work out how much you would lose if the shares were to open at a 10pc discount on the issue price. Then see how much you can afford to lose, and modify your application accordingly. Remember, if it is a dud, you might well get all you ask for, instead of being scaled down.

Some issues do go spectacularly wrong. The Government got caught badly in selling a tranche of BP shares around the October '87 Crash. More recently, shares in Manchester United Football Club slumped from an issue price of 385p to 275p in a few weeks. Villain of the piece was Kevin Maxwell, who dumped over 4pc of the company when dealings began. Shrewd investors, though, were not caught out. They would have read my comments in the *Daily Mail*, explaining exactly why the Manchester United offer was a dud. The prudent punter, even without the Mail, would have sold quickly, once the issue opened, and before the loss got too great. Always cut losses quickly.

OFFERS FOR SALE BY TENDER

So far, I have dealt with tactics for a straightforward offer for sale. Most of them hold good for an offer for sale by tender. That, though, is less attractive. It carries an added complication in that it requires would-be purchasers to determine how much they will pay for the shares. The sponsors set a minimum price, and ask for offers (tenders) above it.

It is permitted, however, to make multiple applications in tender offers, so long as each application is at a different price. So, for example, if the minimum price was 120p, you could apply at 120p, 125p, 130p, 135p and so on – in different amounts at different prices, if you wished.

Once all applications are in, the sponsors set what is called a striking price. All of the shares are sold at that price. Anyone who bids at or above the striking price gets the shares – at the striking price. If you are determined to have some, you can apply at a very high price. If everyone does that, of course, everyone gets the shares at a silly price.

Sponsors choose to sell by tender when they are unsure what price they should set. They can judge the mood more easily, and pick what price they wish, provided they get enough bids above the minimum.

In practice, they will pitch the striking price below the maximum they could have got. They will always want to leave some buyers unsatisfied in the hope of generating a good after-market, with a profit for the stags. Obviously a big bonanza is unlikely. When it comes to judging how much to tender, or whether to play at all, rely on the usual sources – brokers, press, or grey market. But you may well decide not to bother. Offers by tender are inherently less inviting than simple offers for sale.

INTRODUCTIONS

New issues are sometimes brought to market through an introduction. No new shares are on offer, and it is of no interest to the stag. All that happens is that market-makers start quoting prices in shares which are already widely held, but which lacked a listing. Most introductions involve a London quotation for a foreign company.

PLACINGS

Placings are nearly as bad for the stags. The sponsor of a placing fixes the price for shares in a new issue, and can dole them out to a list of applicants. The rules governing who gets them change from time to time. No matter how it is done, it usually means useful profits for a small group, and nothing for the rest. Until the system changes, forget it.

CHAPTER SEVEN
HOW TO PICK A SHARE

It must be easy to make a killing on the stock market, surely? Open any sensible newspaper, and there is a page or two packed with prices, and a stock market report talking about all sorts of juicy gains. Some of the reasons for the rises appear trivial, others absolutely obvious. Of course, the leaders went up when bank base rates went down. No wonder companies which do a lot of business in America improved as the dollar gained ground. No problem, this share picking racket.

Hindsight is wonderful. It makes geniuses of us all. Time after time, I pick up rival papers and read a story I did not write in the Mail. Obvious stuff. I curse myself for being so stupid as to have missed it. It was there for the taking. Next time, I promise myself . . . only to find it has happened again, a few weeks later.

Doing it is different. Actually doing it is difficult. Looking back. you realise how much you knew all along. But you simply did not focus on it. And investment is tough. When you actually have to lay out your own money, it gets much more difficult. Suddenly you realise that there are 7,000 securities of one sort or another to choose from. Some days, the fallers outnumber the risers. The dozen or two movers which make the market reports are not so easy to locate when you look at the price table in the *Financial Times*. It covers two pages, is fearsomely difficult to read, and looks as it it makes no sense at all until you really get the hang of things.

Look more closely, and you find that, even on a good day, almost as many shares may go down as go up. Some newspapers list the numbers. They can be quite a surprise. Even when the market is on a good run, there can be spells when prices drift back day after day. Sometimes, of course, the whole thing turns down, and there is gloom for month after month. But even in the good times, it is easy to lose a fortune by backing a bad business. Or by missing the change of mood when things go off the boil.

Whole sectors can go wrong. In the mid eighties, gullible investors and journalists galore fell in love with advertising agencies. Saatchi & Saatchi grew so over-confident and arrogant that they flirted with taking over the Midland Bank. Martin Sorrell, their old finance director, set up a rival at WPP, and bought some of the most famous names in advertising. Both got it badly wrong. By the end of 1991, both shares were selling for pence rather than several pounds, and struggling desperately. Much the same thing happened to stores, once the stock market darlings. Sir Ralph Halpern left as Burton plunged into crisis, George Davies was fired well before Next hit the bottom, Sir Terence Conran said goodbye to Storehouse, and Gerald Ratner compounded a crash from fat profits into losses by talking about 'crap' in his shops. Not so long before, all looked wonderful winners, making fortunes for themselves and their shareholders.

Steady your nerves, though. Even as recession gripped the economy, relatively few quoted companies actually went bust. Under 40 in 1991, though it seemed like more. The failures always catch the eye. But very few investors lose all of their money. Companies in trouble are usually rescued. And there is rarely any reason why the alert investor should be caught in a real loser. If this book teaches you nothing else, it should show you how to avoid total disaster. The chapter on selling shares – I keep saying it because it is crucial – is the most important in the book.

The arithmetic helps, too. If you lose half of your money, it sounds terrible, but your £1,000 has only gone down to £500, You have lost £500. Double your money, and the £1,000 becomes £2,000. You have made £1,000. In a rising market – and this book is being written in anticipation of a rising market – the chances of doubling your money are much greater than halving it.

It may sound as if I am simply playing with words – halving, doubling, what matters? But the psychological impact of doubling and halving is not to be ignored. If you are going to play the stock market, you have to believe that you will not be daft enough to halve your money too often, and will resolve to sell and limit your loss before you do it. Any investor must believe that there is a fair chance of doubling their money, given a little luck. And in a fair market, that is not asking too much.

AN EXCUSE TO FALL IN LOVE

When you go into the stock market, you are looking for an excuse to fall in love, hunting an investment you can live and grow with. Investing in British industry is the vague kind of notion which everyone thinks makes sense. Thriving companies matter to us as individuals, and as a nation. No matter how much of a gamble it may be in reality, everyone wants it to work.

It is a fine romance, finding the share partner to suit you. City pages parade the temptations before your eyes. You might want to flirt with bid candidates, or get carried away with wild option market favourites. Whatever your fancy, it makes sense to check the fundamentals first. SUCCESSFUL INVESTMENT IS ABOUT ANTICIPATION. You need to spot the attractions before the other investors, and to do that, you need to know the kind of things which appeal to other investors. Top of the list come the dividend yield and the price earnings ratio.

THE DIVIDEND YIELD

Dividend yields form the bedrock of most measured investment decisions. It is no use spotting the next takeover candidate if the bid comes in below the market price (it does happen sometimes) simply because gamblers have got carried away by the bid dream, and have lost touch with investment reality, overvaluing the company.

The dividend yield matters, especially if you are a cautious investor with income high on your list of priorities. Capital gains are super, but dividends roll on year after year, generally growing fatter, no matter what the shares may be doing day by day. That counts a great deal, particularly for older investors who need a good return to bolster their income.

And a consistent and growing stream of dividend income is what the investment giants are seeking. Pension funds and insurance companies are the biggest and most important traders, and influence share prices more than anyone. They take in money today against the promise that they will provide cash at some future date to pensioners and policyholders. They love an investment which will provide them with greater income in future (through dividends). The more secure that income, the better. In many ways, dividend yields drive the whole market. At its crudest, a share is a stake in a business which you hope will earn growing profits so that it can pay higher dividends as time goes by. If there are no dividends, you will get no return from that share until you sell it. Rather like property companies which have grand and glorious empty buildings built on borrowed money, you might have a terrific asset, but the lack of cash flow to pay day to day bills would mean you would go bust without dividends. Just as generating an income is really what determines the capital value of a building to the property company, the stream of dividends ultimately determines the worth of a share.

Bear with me. This may sound obvious and repetitive, but it is a vital investment truth, which easily gets overlooked when markets are hot, and capital values are leaping. In the end, the value of a company to investors is the income it will generate for them. No good having a fabulous mine which will never produce gold to be sold to yield profits to pay dividends. That mine might be given a massive value on the stock market long before anyone digs a serious shaft. But that can only go on for so long. Sooner or later, production and profits will be what counts.

Share investment is essentially about anticipation. In the short term, about anticipating what other investors will do. In the long term, about anticipating the value of the dividends which will flow from the profits a company can produce. No matter how sophisticated the arguments you may get from others, in the very final analysis, that is what matters. Believe me.

The dividend yield is the percentage return from the annual income on a share. Working it out is not difficult. If you are paid £10 a year before tax from an investment which has cost you £100, the yield is 10pc. If you buy 100 shares at £2 each, and the company pays a gross dividend total of 10p a share in the year, the dividend yield is 5pc. You calculate this by taking the total dividend (10p multiplied by 100 shares equal £10), dividing it by total cost (£2 multiplied by 100 shares equals £200), and expressing it as a percentage – 5pc.

The sum is more complicated in reality, because dividends are paid after the deduction of tax. You have to add back the tax before doing the sum. And in the market, they calculate the yield by using not lots of £100, but the cost of just one share, and the dividend on one share. Do not worry about this detail. You need never calculate a dividend yield for yourself. Ask your broker, or look in one of the newspaper share price tables. Most show the yield. Sadly, for space reasons, the *Daily Mail* does not.

As the share price rises, the dividend yield falls, because you are paying more for the same amount of dividend. Conversely, the dividend yield rises as the share price falls, because you are buying the right to the same dividend payment more cheaply. If the dividend is increased, and the share price remains unchanged, the yield goes up. And vice versa. A higher dividend is likely to prompt a higher share price, and a reduced dividend could bring a lower – rather more sharply lower – price.

As a crude guide, the higher the yield, the more risky the share, and the more dubious the prospects of the company. The lower the yield, the higher the market rates prospects of growth. It all goes back to what investors expect profits to do, since they ultimately determine how much money there is to pay dividends.

The market is revising its opinion all of the time, and this is reflected in changing share prices. Sometimes a good company with strong growth prospects will offer a higher yield than others in the same business because few people have realised what is going on. Those shares will be worth buying. On the other hand, a high yield could mean that the City has spotted problems ahead. Profits may be sliding, and the company may not be able to afford such a high dividend by the end of the year. Most published yields are based on dividends paid in the previous year. They may overstate the real yield because the next dividend – the one a new buyer will actually get – could be cut. If the company is doing better, of course, the published yield may be understated, because the dividend could go up.

PINNING YOUR FAITH ON THE PE

Pinning your faith on the price earnings ratio, or the PE, is one of the market's favourite games. Dividend yields have a certain down to earth reality. At the end of the day, you get a dividend cheque through the post, and that means real money in your pocket. The PE means no such thing. It may just be a guess to build a dream on. PE is about mental, not physical, jerks, and is the investment analysts' most powerful piece of ju-ju.

I explained what a PE is in an earlier chapter. Like the dividend yield, it is one of the key tools for comparing one company with another. A high PE means that the market is normally expecting fast profits growth. Or it may mean that a slump is expected this year, and last year's historic PE is out on a limb, ready to be chopped off as profits plunge. Most market rules can be turned on their head. A low PE usually means lower profits or poor growth are anticipated. Unless, that is, you know better. You may just have spotted a company with high growth potential and a low PE. Then you may have found a barrgain. Take it to your heart – after trying to make sure you, not the market, are not the one making a terrible mistake. The market does not get things that wrong that often, but it does happen.

VARIATIONS ON A THEME

Different strokes for different folks. The dividend yield or the PE appropriate to one sector, one industry, may not be right for another. Sometimes the market decides it has gone wrong, and a whole sector is re-rated, up or down. Sometimes the different ratings make obvious sense. In 1986, it was hard to argue with lower PEs and higher dividend yields for oil stocks than for stores. They reflected the uncertain prospects for oil profits against the background of chaos in OPEC. Consumer spending was soaring, and profit prospects for most of the High Street looked wonderful. After the 1987 slump, of course, that changed. Oil shares did not win higher ratings, but the swift players began to dump stores, starting a slide which continued well into the nineties as profits collapsed.

Fashion plays a prominent role in investment ratings. It is easy to get sucked in, so try to keep your feet on the ground. City backroom boys do get it wrong, and get carried away by dreams of glory for different industries. We all ought to have appreciated in the eighties that the personal computer boom would go bust – and it did. Simple common sense should have told anyone that the chance of such fat early profits would bring a flood of competition from new entrants, bringing everyone's profit margins tumbling down.

In the wake of the 1987 Crash, I tired of telling people to sell property shares, because it was clear that the City was headed for hard times, and would not be able to afford ridiculous expansion plans using expensive new offices. It was no great shakes in the forecasting stakes – simple common sense. That is a commodity which often eludes City aces as they run with the pack. Living in each other's pockets, they are easily fooled when booming profit prospects are on the lips of everyone in every wine bar within half a mile of Throgmorton Street. That is why some of the best investment managers are based in Scotland. They pride themselves on being detached from the silly gossip, above it all, able to take an objective view. There is something in it.

Equally, however, it does not do to be too smart. It hurts to recall the profit opportunities I missed, and the wonderful tips I could have given *Daily Mail* readers in the eighties had I not been so cautious. Time and again, I looked at companies on the move, and recognised old tricks and dubious names from the early seventies. Because I thought I could spot what was happening, I kept away, quietly forecasting problems ahead. Often, I was right. Sooner or later, so many of the suspect little games, the brief fashionable stocks, fell apart. But by keeping aloof, I had missed profit opportunities galore while the game was still good. Before the problems, there would often be 18 months or more of glorious short-term gains.

You need to know what fashions are in, and when to go with them. If you can spot the emerging trend early enough, no matter how suspect, it can yield handsome returns – provided you get out before the mood changes. You can be too smart, too cautious, for your own good. My smug satisfaction at spotting the dubious nature of many situations was spoilt when I woke up to how well others had done by playing along with the games.

EYEING THE AVERAGES

Keep a hold on reality by eyeing the averages. The best place to find them is in the *Financial Times*. Each day it carries a detailed table headed 'FT-ACTUARIES SHARE INDICES'. It moves about the paper a bit, but is usually near the stock market report. This splits the market into 70 or more groups, and gives the average dividend yield, and PE, plus other odds and ends for each group, and the market as a whole. That way you can compare, say, the yield and PE on National Westminster Bank with the average for all of the main shares in the bank sector.

Obviously these continually shift with market moves. But if you spot one sector which is way out of line, be extra cautious. You will need a very good reason for investing in it. All too often, it means shares in that particular industry have run too far ahead. They will be pulled back in line not by a roaring boom, but by a slump – in profits, or in share prices. Since the market always tends to overdo things – up or down – that could mean dramatic losses. Similar reservations apply if you spot an individual share way out of line with the average for the group.

PROSPECTIVE PROBLEMS

Be wary, too, of ambitious projections. In a rising market, those who once considered PE ratios of 15 rather racy soon learn to live with them, and begin to feel comfortable with PEs in the 20s.

Look hard. As the mood gets merrier, you may find you have switched from talking about historic PEs based on actual profits companies have already made, to prospective PEs, based on what this year's profits might be – altogether more speculative sums based on guesses, a little trip into the unknown.

Any price earnings ratio in excess of 25 needs a special explanation, and should only be attached to a very special company indeed. Of the familiar UK names, only Body Shop appears to be able to command an astronomic rating almost indefinitely – though I would be careful. It is growing big enough and international enough to meet the kind of organisational problems which confront all majors, and may cause a real slowdown in growth. The high PE warning applies no matter what the averages, no matter how buoyant the market. If PEs over 25 become common, it is a clear warning that the market is getting overheated.

Early in 1986, otherwise sane and respectable fund managers were beginning to cite prospective price earnings ratios based on projected profits for 1990. They might have been right. They might have been mad. Either way, if they believed they were basing decisions on anything other than sheer guesswork, they were fooling themselves. It is impossible to make a sensible forecast for more than two years ahead. The imponderables are just too great.

ASSET BACKING – THE BACKSTOP

Once you are satisfied that the dividend yield and price earnings ratio makes sense in the share of your choice, check the asset backing. This is the backstop. It gives you an idea of what the company might fetch if it stopped trading, the business was sold, and the borrowings repaid.

Assets were described earlier when we discussed the balance sheet. To discover the asset backing of a company, take the total value of assets – land, buildings, machinery, stocks, cash and such – deduct the liabilities – loans, tax due, creditors and so on – and you get shareholders' funds. Divide this sum by the number of Ordinary shares in issue, and you have net asset backing per share. As usual, this is not something you have to calculate yourself. A few companies actually publish it in their annual report. But your broker will check it for you.

Asset backing is not too important day to day. What matters most is the profits earned from those assets. No-one bothered much about the asset backing of Imperial Chemical

Industries until Hanson picked up a small stake and began hovering as a possible bidder. Even then, in a company like ICI, trading profits continued to be the main issue. But assets can be important where there is the chance of a bid, and these days there are precious few companies where you can rule out the possibility. So it is always comforting to know that the share of your choice can lay claim to a fat pile of assets. That can be crucial if a company is in trouble, or in one of two specialist categories – property companies or investment trusts.

Obviously the more assets, the better. The closer those assets are to cash, the better. Look in the balance sheet to find the cash (minus overdrafts), or investments (saleable shares in other companies). There may also be a holding in an unquoted associate company. That may be in the books at a nominal value, but might be worth a great deal more if sold. Property usually comes next in the asset line-up, though in the nineties it is a much more dubious benefit. The nearer London the better used to be the rule, and the older the date of valuation, the more scope there could be for greater value than the figures suggest. In the early nineties, though, any property needs to be treated with caution. Valuations from the late eighties or early nineties could prove optimistic, especially if they relate to offices in London.

Plant and machinery values are always doubtful. Though listed as an asset, much of it may be virtually worthless in a sale. Stocks (whatever the company makes, or the raw materials it makes them from) are also of uncertain worth. Clearly last year's fashions are not worth much to a clothing company, nor Ninja Turtle toys when the 1990 boom was over.

Pay particular attention to debtors, the negative side of the balance sheet. You must be scrupulous in knocking off the full weight of loans in calculating asset value, and you should ALWAYS ASSUME THE WORST. If a loan has to be redeemed by the company under any circumstances, deduct the full cost of repayment. The worst has an uncanny knack of coming to the worst, just when you can least afford it.

Ideally, you want a company which is trading well, with an asset backing comfortably in excess of the share price. Then you are covered both ways – either the shares sell as a promising trading situation, or someone might take a fancy to the company and make a bid to take over the assets and put them to better use where they can earn more profits.

Such companies can be hard to find, though if you get in before the share boom gathers steam, there will be plenty about. The strongest asset situations crop up when a company has had a trading setback, and the price has fallen. Disappointing profits often leave assets looking cheap. You have to decide whether the setback is temporary, and whether those assets are worthwhile. That is not easy, but at least if you pick an asset-backed recovery company, asset power will help you sleep more easily.

THE ASSET EXCEPTIONS – PROPERTY COMPANIES AND INVESTMENT TRUSTS

Shares in property companies and investment trusts usually sell for less than the value of their assets – a discount. In bad times, the discount can be as large as 60pc in the case of property companies, and 35pc for investment trusts – though, once again, there can be exceptions. This means you could find a property company with 100p of assets with shares at 40p or less, or an investment trust with 100p of assets whose shares are 65p.

Do not get carried away thinking you have found a bargain. The City will know about it, and there will be a good reason for it. Brokers have vast expensive teams of analysts specialising in different sectors. They do nothing else but look at property shares or investment trusts.

Large property share discounts will reflect worries about the viability of the company, and the accuracy of their last published valuations. In the early nineties, property companies led the list of collapses. Time and again, they were saddled with enormous buildings which they could not let. No-one wanted to rent them. Empty buildings are not just a useless asset. They are expensive, depreciating assets – or, rather, nasty liabilities. An empty property is costly to keep in good condition. It needs guarding, and the systems must be kept in working order. It will almost certainly have been built with borrowed money, and that will be racking up interest charges every minute.

At one stage, companies were offering rent free periods, even paying people to use their properties, just to reduce the cost of outgoings. Until properties have a tenant, and an assured flow of rental income, their capital value is debatable. The quality of the rent roll, and the amount of the rents, really determines what someone will pay to buy a building, given that most of the buyers are insurance companies or pension funds looking for a predictable flow of rising income as time goes by.

In the early nineties, there was a surplus of empty properties, and a great millstone of debt around the necks of most property companies. Their asset valuations were dubious, to put it kindly. There will be investment opportunities among property companies in the coming share boom, but it is a sector to be treated with great caution until you can be pretty sure you know what you are doing. Stay away.

Investment trusts are altogether different. As explained earlier, they hold shares in other companies, quoted or unquoted. They hope to boost revenue by picking companies whose dividends are growing. And they hope to boost their own capital value by picking companies whose shares are rising.

A number of stockbrokers have departments which follow every nuance, and can calculate the slightest change in underlying asset value of the trusts day by day. County Natwest and Warburg Securities are probably the best. You will not be able to compete against such people in discovering any new excitement. But you can do well by going with the flow, choosing shares in sectors which are making headway.

It is also worth paying attention to the investments which the trusts themselves make. Most will be delighted to send you their latest report and accounts. The best provide a complete list of their holdings, plus a thumb-nail sketch of what those companies do, and why they are worth supporting. That way, you can get useful tips from some of the best-paid professionals in the investment world.

READING THE CITY PAGES

It is all very well arming yourself with the standard tools – dividend yield, PE, and asset value – but everyone can get them. They merely give you an investment road map. You must decide where you are going, and how you are going to get there. You must add that touch of your own, the extra ingredient which will make a particular share the right investment for you.

You need to develop a feel for the market. Try to immerse yourself in it as far as possible. You need to develop the trading instinct which will ultimately be your most important asset – except, perhaps, sheer luck. But we all know about luck. The harder you work, the luckier you get.

The simply way of getting a feel for what is happening is to read the City pages regularly. Pay particular attention to the stock market report. The *Financial Times*, the *Independent* and the *Daily Mail* are among the best. What you really want to know is not so much what happened yesterday, but what might happen next.

Most market reports carry unconfirmed gossip. Some is rubbish, plain and simple. Some of it is remarkably well informed. Few market reporters are experienced analysts. They are poorly equipped to make decisions on what is good and what is bad. They rely on whoever they speak to. Market reporters are often fed stories by people who simply want to set a share moving, up or down, because they have a position in it themselves. Some reports carry stories as a favour for past information, some because they know no better.

PUBLIC RELATIONS

Much of the gossip is planted by public relations agents employed by public companies. Some agencies work for dozens of companies. They leak stories unofficially, using the press to manipulate the market. Others simply like to impress their clients with the sheer volume of comment they can generate. Rarely do they drop bad news to journalists. Sometimes, though, they leak a diluted version to soften up market expectations of something really grim. Just now and then they leak really bad tidings so that an otherwise shocking result will not appear quite so bad when it comes. Usually, however, they give a hint of something good to come.

Both sides think they benefit. The reporter has a little story which may move the shares the next day, making him look good. The public relations agent thinks he has done his client a good turn. It may be deplorable manipulation, but it cannot be disregarded, because it does move prices. So you have to pay heed to it, with a suitably cynical perspective.

In the longer run, the whole thing can be dubious. It results in news being fed to a limited audience, and often interpreted in misleading fashion. It can prompt naive investors to buy on a tip which should never have seen the light of day.

Keep such reservations in mind when you read the market reports. And do not forget them when you go on to the rest of the City pages. You will soon find who suits you best, who makes the most sense. Some Sunday pages are particularly prone to running friendly stories on companies fed to them by public relations agents. They need to fill the space somehow. Do not disregard them, however. The good news will often turn out to be true, and leaking it indicates which shares are being powered by a public relations push. That means someone is working to get them higher – no bad thing if treated with suitable caution.

Some journalists are especially gullible. All make mistakes. My most glaring error was to recommend Polly Peck a few months before the crash. Once his sternest critic, I had become a firm friend of chairman Asil Nadir through the years, and believed in his plans. I passed them on to *Daily Mail* readers in the form of share recommendations, usually with great success. Sadly, I did not spot the potential problems. To this day, I am ready to apologise to any readers who took my mistaken advice.

Hopefully, my attitude makes sense. Financial journalists bear a heavy responsibility to readers, one which some of them do not discharge with credit. On the whole, though, most journalists try honestly to convey what they believe to be the proper story. Rarely do they know anything approaching the whole truth. But financial journalists are important to investors. They may be ignorant, careless, and easily-fooled. But they are the only genuinely independent source of advice most people can get. Most other sources of advice have a financial interest in the advice they give. So stick with the press. It may be better than you think.

The *Financial Times* carries the most weight. It covers virtually every item of company and economic news, and frequently interprets it usefully. The 'Lex' column is required City reading, and can move shares sharply. It varies in quality as the contributors change – a problem which influences all newspapers. The *Daily Mail* City section is widely accepted as a sharper, more readable companion to the *Financial Times*. It mixes gossip, news and opinion freely in a fashion few others follow. It is closer to the chat you might hear over lunch in the City. My contributions have always been heavily slanted towards the private investor. I am always eager to learn of examples worth fighting for – though the pressure of helping produce a page each day means that I do not reply to letters as often as I should. I am sorry. But do tell me what upsets you – I take comments from readers seriously.

The *Daily Telegraph* is a consistently intelligent commentator, enlivened by the wit of Christopher Fildes. *The Independent* is valuable. Among Sunday papers, *The Observer* is intelligently aggressive, led by the foraging of Michael Gillard. He contributes to the *Private*

Eye column 'City Slicker', one of the most important in financial journalism. It has some of the best City scandal-mongering, though it may not always be accurate.

Pick your own tipsters. Be wary of the little snippets mentioning several companies. These tend to adopt a shotgun approach, allowing the papers to proclaim their tipping abilities. The many misses are quietly forgotten, and much of the material is pumped in by public relations people.

UNDERSTANDING THE PRICE TABLES

The most comprehensive price table is in the *Financial Times*. Understanding it has become harder since the format was changed towards the end of 1991, and finding individual prices can be a nightmare. Read the accompanying notes carefully, however, and it can be deciphered.

It tells you an impressive amount about each company. There is the middle price, the amount of any change, the high and low for the past year or so, the dividend yield, the PE, and the market capitalisation. There are also blobs and notes of different sorts, with the blobs purporting to mark the most actively traded stocks. This does not always appear to be as accurate as it might be. In the 'Investment Trusts' section there is also a figure for net asset value (NAV), and a column to show the discount or premium reflected in the share price.

All of the broadsheets carry prices, some with numbers for phone lines which can be used during the day to get the latest price. On a Saturday, the *Financial Times* also lists actual share markings. This covers rule 535 trading and other special areas, and can be useful in picking up some more obscure stocks whose prices are not readily available elsewhere.

MARKET CAPITALISATION

Market capitalisation is invaluable. It shows the value of the whole company, worked out by multiplying the number of shares in issue by the price. In an instant, it gives you an idea whether you are talking about the kind of company which has to be taken seriously, or a tiddler which could be vulnerable in hard times, or might rocket when the mood is right.

It is amazing how often enthusiasm comes crashing to earth when you realise that some would-be winner is already valued at millions more than you might have expected – or a would-be bidder is so small that it could not possibly launch the bid that the rumours suggest. Some little ones do make offers for their bigger brethren, but normally the bidder needs to be at least as big as the target company.

ALL THE EXES

The price tables are scattered with cryptic exes. They are ex dividend, ex scrip, ex rights. The ex means 'without'. If you buy a share ex dividend (or xd), it means that you are not buying the right to a recent dividend which was declared by the company, but which has not yet been sent out. Ex scrip (or ex cap, or merely xc) means you buy without the right to a recent scrip issue. And ex rights (or xr) means the shares are no longer entitled to subscribe to a recent rights issue.

You are not losing by these exes. Share prices will have been adjusted to reflect the loss of these benefits. Sometimes prices seem to fall sharply, but if you look more closely, you will find that they have simply gone 'ex' something. For example, share which are ex a one for one scrip issue will halve in price, because there will be twice as many of them from that point. The opposite to ex is cum (meaning 'with'). That means you do buy the shares with the rights to a dividend, scrip, or rights issue.

RECENT ISSUES

Several papers carry a table of recent issues, but the *Financial Times* has the best. It covers the price of shares in new issues, or rights issue. It offers a handy guide to the premium on shares which are trading ex rights – telling you how much you could get if you wanted to sell your entitlement to a rights issue from a company where you are a shareholder. It can be attractive to buy these rights entitlements. They give you a way of buying in at relatively low dealing cost, or the opportunity for a low cost short term speculation.

There is a short period – a few weeks usually – when these rights to subscribe to a rights issue are tradeable. If, say, a company launches a one for two rights issue at 100p when the shares are 120p, the rights will be worth, in theory, be worth just over 13p. That can be calculated by taking the price of two shares at 120p, plus another at 100p, so that after the rights issue you have three shares which have cost 340p, or just over 113p each. So the value of your rights share is not the 100p you have to pay, but 113p.

If the shares move up in the market to 124p, a relatively modest gain, then the rights are worth 16p, a rise of almost a quarter. You calculate it by taking two shares at 124p, plus one at 100p. That equals 348p. Divide it by three to get 116p, or 16p above the price of the rights at 100p. You can see there are opportunities for fast, fat profits.

But it is high-risk investment. Look at what happens if the share price proper goes down. A fall from 120p to 116p means the rights are worth under 11p (two times 116p equals 232p, plus 100p, equals 332p. Divide 332p by three equals just under 111p, minus 100p). The fall from just under 13p (when the shares were 120p) to just under 11p means a hefty percentage loss. It is not a game to play until you have resources you can afford to risk, know a good, helpful broker, and fully understand what you are doing.

HIGHS AND LOWS

Once again, the *Financial Times* has the best list giving shares which hit highs and lows for the past year in the previous trading session. Study it. Sometimes it can be frustrating. On a day when the market surges or slumps, there can be too many new highs and lows for individual names to be listed. When they are there, though, they form a useful way of picking up movers you may have missed from simply scanning the market report or the main changes. They show the shares which are quietly moving along.

Many changes will be prompted by readily accessible announcements. Others will be more subtle. They will be sparked by quiet insider dealing, people in the know buying or selling. Or by changes in broker profit forecasts. Or by a buying programme from someone building a share stake.

Watch especially for those moving against the trend, shares which rise on a dull day, or fall when the market is good. Those are usually more than just casual moves. They will have a special reason. It is tempting to think that by the time shares have hit the highs or lows list, you have missed the main action. Not so. The trend is your friend, they say. If the shares have broken into new ground, the chances are that they will keep moving that way a while longer.

They will start interesting others who watch the high and low lists. And once a share reaches new territory, that can have additional impact, as I explain later in dealing with chartists.

TRADING VOLUME

The latest addition to the investors' armoury is a table in the *Financial Times* labelled 'Trading Volume in Major Stocks'. Something like it does appear elsewhere, and is well worth studying. Sadly, it still only covers some 200 leading companies. It can be misleading. Sometimes deals are inaccurately recorded, and sometimes they are done outside the system, or in a fashion deliberately designed to escape the net. Bear in mind, too, that the real number changing hands will be half the figure published. That figure takes in the sale and the purchase, so there is double counting.

Nonetheless, the table is a useful indication of the weight of money behind particular changes. Clearly a 2p rise on volume of 50,000 shares is less comforting than one on volume of 500,000 shares – but only in some ways. We come back to the snag of being able to interpret almost any rule in conflicting fashion.

A big rise on small trading volume might be suspect. It could be a freak, sparked because the market-maker was caught short of stock, something which may not last long. Or it could mean the market is fragile, and the price will respond quickly and dramatically to modest buying – ideal for a quick profit. Existing investors might all be firm holders, determined not to sell. Excellent. Or it could mean that if a sizeable seller comes on, there will not be buyers enough for the stock, and the price will plummet.

Sometimes you will see heavy volume of four million shares or so, and hardly any price change. Buyers and sellers evenly matched, not much point in picking them up, because it will take a mighty change in attitude to move the price? Perhaps.

Heavy is a relative term. Regular trades of one million shares or more mean little on most days in ICI, Hanson, or the likes. But they would be big news for something like RMC, the building materials supplier. And do not forget the money involved. Trading 11m shares in supermarkets group Asda at 32p involves perhaps £1.7m. Three million shares in National Westminster Bank at 270p means over £4m has changed hands.

When markets were booming, some investors followed a variation on a plan devised by Nicholas Darvas, a former dancer (*How I Made $2,000,000 in the Stock Market*). He explained how he made his fortune in America by combining price moves with volume. The higher the volume when shares are rising, the better. The system looks appealing, but is is hampered by the lack of easily accessible volume figures. You can, however, ask your broker to check them for you by using his SEAQ Level Two screen.

EQUITY FUTURES AND OPTIONS TRADING

Moves in the real market are influenced increasingly by positions in the futures market. This is a fast-moving area dominated by professional players. From time to time, futures are used to manipulate the main market, and vice versa. The *Financial Times* has the best report of what goes on.

Traditional options are gradually being elbowed aside. I deal later with how they can be used for profit, but as a general guide, they can yield ideas for specific investment. Watch the list. Broadly speaking, call options mean someone expects a rise of 20pc or more over the next three months, while a put suggests a fall. Double options mean they expect action, but are not sure whether it will be good or bad. That, though, is a vast over-simplification. Watch the list more as a way of pointing up stocks which are worth investigation, simply because some other punter is taking an interest in them. And who knows what they may know?

WHAT THE BROKERS SAY

Some newspapers and magazines carry regular slots summarising a few of the circulars sent out by leading stockbrokers. The *Daily Mail* has been featuring a list on Saturdays or Mondays. The *Investors Chronicle* has one every week. They are worth watching, simply to see what well-informed City chaps are saying. By the time they reach the press, they are often out of date. But since they influence the market, they are important. It might be worth ringing the broker concerned for a copy of what takes your fancy. The broker might not let you have one, but some will.

Some circulars are remarkably detailed and well-informed. Others? Well, we all have our problems – and some brokers, of course, will be closely linked to the company whose shares they are praising. Make a special point of trying to check whether they are the 'shop', or broker to the company.

INVESTMENT MAGAZINES

There is only one investment magazine of consequence – the *Investors Chronicle*. Weekly, it is almost essential reading. It combines general articles with features on particular companies and industries, covers anything from economics to option trading. Most useful of all are the brief analytical pieces in the second half, commenting on almost all company announcements, and analysing each new set of accounts. These analyses give a handy statement of asset values, and borrowing levels. IC opinions are sometimes off beam, but for the serious investor, the magazine is excellent.

Money Observer is monthly, and a valuable source of much solid information. Others like *What Investment* or *Moneywise* are more erratic, and of limited value. Their share tips, in particular, should be approached with extreme caution.

TIP SHEETS

Tip sheets – investment newsletters – can be worthwhile. The most prominent is the *Fleet Street Letter*. It is quite racy, but usually backed by thoughtful research, and good sense. Watch for offers of cut-price subscriptions which it runs every so often. The *IC Newsletter*, linked to the *Investors Chronicle*, has been relaunched as the *Investors Stockmarket Letter*. It needed revamping, and the new team has a good pedigree. They are involved in an impressive, but expensive publication called *Analyst*.

Penny Share Guide and *Penny Share Focus* are also worth considering if you are seeking a gamble. They produce so many interesting ideas that it is easy to think you should be spreading your cash everywhere in small doses, fearful of missing the next winner. All of the tip sheets spot some goodies, and find it easier to forget their flops. Use them as a source of possible ideas, and as a way of teaching yourself what to look out for, not as a bible to be taken totally seriously. I should declare an interest – the Chartsearch company which publishes some tip sheets has published hard-back copies of some of my investment books. *Penny Share Focus* has been advertising my book *How To Make A Killing In Penny Shares* for some time.

Market-makers subscribe to all of the tip sheets, so tip prices are usually marked up smartly before actual trading opens, and there can be a scramble to buy when the market is hot. So subscribers often pay over the odds, and might do better to wait a day or two for the temperature to cool. Some newsletters are too slow to advise subscribers when to sell. Nonetheless, a good newsletter can be worth taking when fun is in the air. Beware of newsletters which are circulated free of charge. These are meant to lure you into buying something or other. Often they create the opening which gives some dodgy share pusher an excuse to phone you. Have absolutely nothing to do with them, especially any from overseas. Better still, send me a copy so that I can warn *Daily Mail* readers off.

Steer clear, too, of telephone share tipping lines. These attract a flurry of interest among the City professionals, who have to know what is being pushed to the mug punters. They may appear well in touch with events, but I am very uneasy about them. And they are expensive.

ORACLE ON THE TV

If you have a TV set with Teletext, you might find the Oracle pages useful. They come free of charge, and provide a handy City news service throughout the day. It covers everything from share prices to foreign exchange rates and company announcements. It is far from comprehensive, and lags behind events, but is a useful stopgap for investors stranded at home.

OTHER SOURCES

Where else can you go for clues? Your local library, for a start. Check the reference shelves, the stock of newspapers and magazines. You might find some surprising new sources of information. If, for example, the investment love of your life should be a supermarket company, cast an eye over *The Grocer*. It could give you valuable tips about what is happening, who looks good, and who is full of ideas, opening in new places.

Trade papers often beat the national press to stories in their own specialist areas. Now and then, they could put you on to a real winner before the rest of the world wakes up. On the *Daily Mail*, we picked up several price-sensitive stories on Eurotunnel from the construction press. The bigger the library, the wider the range of useful publications.

Major libraries also carry Extel cards. These are produced by the Exchange Telegraph Company, and serve as standard reference sources for many stockbrokers, big investors, and newspaper offices. There is an Extel card for every public company, and additional services covering major private companies (useful when a public company is rumoured to be taking over someone private), and foreign companies.

The cards may look complicated, but will repay a little patience. They tell you what the company does, its address, the name and address of the registrars (who keep records of all shareholdings), plus a list of main subsidiary companies. They also show who is on the board, the main shareholders, how the price has moved over the years, what the balance sheet looks like, the net asset value, dividend details, and potted versions of recent announcements. The cards are updated regularly.

Extel cards are a number-cruncher's delight, though you should not get carried away. They record the past, and what matters to you is the future.

Libraries may also carry the Stock Exchange Weekly Official Intelligence. That lists all share quotations, plus a variety of odds and ends. Most useful is the list of dealings by directors. The Stock Exchange Official Yearbook may also be there. That has basic information, company names and addresses, brief profits, and so on.

There could be some of the reference books which cover similar ground to Extel cards. They are relatively expensive, and will not be worth buying unless you are a totally dedicated dealer – and then they will probably become out of date too quickly for you. They include the Extel Handbook of Market Leaders, and the Hambro Company Guide.

If you work in the City, there is a specialised business library, which is well worth a lunch-time trip. The librarians are very helpful, and there is an enormous range of specialist publications.

Then come the companies themselves. Never hesitate to write to any which take your fancy. Check the registered address on an Extel card or in the Stock Exchange Yearbook, and ask the company secretary for the latest report and accounts. Almost invariably, you will get a helpful reply.

Watch, too, for newspaper advertisements of company progress. And pay attention to unit trust and investment trust advertisements. See which areas are in vogue, and watch where the money is flowing.

Write to the more successful fund managers (most family finance pages run league tables regularly). They will send reports and brochures which will show what they have been buying and selling.

You can pick the brains of all manner of investment experts for the price of a postage stamp. An inventive investor need never feel alone out there. There is always a queue of City professionals seeking to impress you, and sell you their services. Just remember – they get it wrong sometimes, too.

CHAPTER EIGHT
SHARE PERSONALITIES

The deeper you delve, the more you get sucked into the market, the more you find that shares are not simply boring bits of paper. They come alive. Companies and their share prices have very distinct personalities. Some you will like, others you will loathe. Try to step back and rationalise it, rather than letting it sneak up on you. Otherwise, one morning you might wake to realise you are sitting on a load of rubbish, a share portfolio which is simply not suited to what you are trying to achieve.

BUILDING A PORTFOLIO

Conventional wisdom will tell you to spread your investments to reduce your risk. No share can be absolutely safe, and the most unexpected things can, and do, happen. If you hold ten different shares, the chances of them all going wrong are modest, though if the whole market collapses, they could all suffer. Within that ten, you ought to have a mix of industries – not all stores or engineers, for instance. While you might be able to afford the odd small, speculative company, it is best to balance it with a solid chunk of major names, which are less likely to spring any nasty surprises.

That sort of advice would win a nod of approval from most investment advisers. Build a portfolio with a sensible, conservative profile. That is the way to do it. And yet . . . And yet that may not suit you at all. How can you spread your risk if you have £1,000 or £2,000 to play with? It makes no sense to split £2,000 between ten companies. And £1,000? No way. Dealing costs would eat up an enormous portion of your cash.

Even if you have the money to spread wider – say £1,000 each in ten shares – that may not suit your temperament. Picking one decent share is hard enough, let alone finding ten. One or two winners, even if they double, would not make that much of an impression on a £10,000 portfolio. Turning £10,000 into £12,000 is very nice. But it hardly sparkles with sex appeal, does it?

Through the years, I have formed the impression that many private investors want excitement. They are prepared to gamble with a modest amount of capital, taking a high risk here and there, hoping for a high return – the Polly Peck dream, if you like, where £2,500 was transformed into £1 million in three years – if you bought at the right time, held on, and sold at the right time.

Perhaps you are ready to take more of a gamble than the experts suggest. If you really are using money you can afford to lose – and you should certainly view your first foray into the stock market as a potential losing proposition – you might be more inclined to split your £2,000 between just two companies, or even your £10,000 between three or four. That would mean a worthwhile return if you did pick a winner.

Do not let me tempt you. My inclination is towards the more aggressive approach. You can play anyway you wish. Decide for yourself. That is what matters. Do not let anyone tell you what to do with your money. Whether you really like the thought or not, stock market money is gambling money. You can play it wild, or you can play it carefully. Just so long as you are realistic, and acknowledge to yourself what you are really doing.

BLUE CHIPS

Blue chips are the cream of the crop, shares in the biggest, best and safest companies. Marks & Spencer, British Telecom, Prudential Assurance, Imperial Chemical Industries, Great Universal Stores, those sort of names. The list changes from time to time. Every so often, even the odd blue chip gets a little cracked. At one stage, National Westminster Bank was on the list. These days, like all clearing banks, it has made so many foolish loans and dissipated so much capital that it can hardly be held up as a model to anyone.

Blue chips are likely to have a market capitalisation in excess of £1bn, and if all of the names are not immediately familiar, they will own companies whose names are well-known. It is possible to deal easily in large quantities of the shares of such companies. Market-makers routinely quote prices in 50,000, maybe 100,000 without altering the price. A million or two might change hands each day, many more when times are busy. Because of that, trading in them is relatively cheap, with a narrow spread between buying and selling prices. Because they are so well-established, pillars of the investment community, they are widely assumed to be safe. Can't go wrong with them, old chap.

Or can you? They got the blue chip name from the highest-value chips in a poker game, and they can be quite a gamble. The price of Marks & Spencer moved between 213p and 301p in 1991. British Telecom between 268p and 423p, the Pru between 187p and 266p, ICI between 845p and 1381p, and GUS between 1048p and 1455p.

Those figures do not necessarily represent the extremes of what you could have made or lost. They did not move straight from the bottom to the top, or vice versa. But they do suggest that, even in a year when the market was relatively good and fairly serene, there are sharp movements. ICI, for example, spent all year below the £16 it touched in 1987, despite speculation over a bid from Hanson.

By and large, though, the lower-risk reputation is well-earned. Blue chips are safer than the average share, less likely to let you down. They have a history of building their business carefully and responsibly. They are well researched throughout the City. Everyone knows the broad direction of their business and their profits. They may not always go up, but if they are going to rise or fall sharply, everyone gets the message in good time to prepare for it. Though increasing US involvement in our markets can lead to sharper price changes, they tend to move in fairly steady, predictable lines. Everyone has ample room to think carefully, to buy or sell without undue haste. No-one will tell you that buying a blue chip was a bad mistake, even if you lose money on it. And you can sleep safe.

HIGH INCOME SHARES

This book is slanted towards capital growth, rather than high income situations. Fixed interest investments offer the highest return, but normally lack the capital gains potential to resist the steady drip of inflation, which gradually erodes the worth of capital.

High income shares, however, combine a good return with the chance of some capital gain. Spotting the high return is relatively easy, though picking an all-round winner is far tougher. Look down the list of dividend yields, decide what return you want, and place strong emphasis on high profits and dividend cover. The greater the cover – the amount by which profits available for distribution exceed the cost of paying the dividend – the further profits can fall before a company is forced to cut the dividend. Safety counts a lot with income stocks.

Unfortunately, the highest income shares are the riskiest. The yield may be high because it might not be there tomorrow. Always view a 10pc plus yield with suspicion. In 1986, the fattest yields were in gold and oil shares. The dangers were obvious, with South Africa in turmoil, and the price of oil in retreat. By 1991, the high yielders were housebuilders and property shares – sectors deep in trouble with companies collapsing all around.

It is always worth looking at investment trusts for a high return. Where you see a trust with two or three classes of share, you will find high-yielding income shares. These come with the split-level trusts, clever little schemers which credit most of the capital growth from the shares they hold to a special class of capital share, while granting almost all of the income from their investments to their own income shares.

Be warned, though. There are often special conditions attached to split-level shares. The income shares, for instance, may be redeemable at a set date for little more than their nominal value. That might involve a capital loss which would reduce the value of the earlier high income. Do not shy away. Take advice from investment trust specialists.

Shrewdly selected high income shares can outperform a growth portfolio on occasion, especially when income is taken into account. On total return, high yield unit trusts frequently come near the top of the charts. In an uncertain market, shares with a high yield are presented as having defensive qualities. The slightly dubious notion is that their greater dividend return will prevent them falling as far as higher fliers with only a tiny return. When the going gets tough, investors concentrate on dividend yields as a surer thing than capital growth.

It sounds plausible, and has some merit. In practice, however, the income prop can get knocked away. Companies do cut dividends, and when the whole market is falling, good goes down with bad. Higher-yielders fall with the rest, and the market looks for higher returns from everything. Income stocks may not fall as far as out-of-favour growth stocks, but fall they will. It is little consolation that you may be losing less than the next investor. You will still end up down. And that is not the idea.

Where high income shares do well, they do it for the classic reason – the higher the risk, the greater the return. If they come right, the capital gain is heavier. So when you opt for a high income buy – outside the fixed interest sector – you may be taking on a riskier proposition than you realise. Do it with your eyes open. Unless you know better – and are sure of it – higher return almost invariably does mean higher risk.

That brings us back to the beginning of this chapter, and spreading risk. If you really do want a high return, you ought to try to spread your risk as far as you sensibly can. Do not plunge all on one or two stocks. Try to find half a dozen high-yielders, just in case one goes wrong. You must appreciate, though, that one dud, if it happens, will cost you enough to knock a point or two off your overall return. So the high yield might not be that tempting after all.

GROWTH STOCKS

Growth stocks are heavenly bodies, investments everybody dreams about, shares that go on and up supported by a busy board and ever-expanding profits. You never intend, of course, to buy anything else. After all, you are not laying your money down to see it sit and do nothing. You could get that in the building society.

The growth stock commands a higher price earnings ratio than average, and gives a lower dividend yield. The idea is that you accept lower returns today in exchange for growth tomorrow. Such stocks need to be in fashionable industries, run by fashionably alert directors, ready to expand by organic growth and by acquisition.

Growth stocks are not always what they seem. Great Universal Stores, for example, has long appeared to be the slumbering giant of the mail order catalogue and the High Street. It hardly ranks as fashionable. Yet it has a record of around 40 years of unbroken growth in profits. Beauty, though, is in the eye of the beholder, and not too many trendy eyes have glanced the way of GUS through the years. Those which do more often see a company with two classes of capital, and the chance of greater growth when votes are more evenly distributed and Wolfson family control weakens.

Expansion by acquisition is one of the key elements in the growth game. It can mean frequent issues of highly rated shares, perhaps supplemented by increased borrowings to mix a little cash in with any takeover bait.

The idea is that a company with a price earnings ratio of 20 can gobble up one on a PE of 10, and gain a fresh injection of growth. If both are the same size, a price earnings ratio of 10 merged with one of 20 will produce a company with a price earnings ratio of 15. Mix in the notion that the two together can save costs, and apply the premium talents of a growth stock management team to the lowly-rated acquisition, and suddenly the City can be persuaded that a PE of 15 is too modest for this exciting new and larger animal. It should really sell on a PE of what? Shall we say 18? Shall we say 20, given a little time? So the shares perk up, and the game can start again after a pause for digestion. It is wonderful how a PE play like that, hatched on the back of an envelope, can start a minor industrial revolution, rationalising British industry and all that – with a profit or two for bankers, brokers, directors and share punters along the way.

Using highly rated shares as currency is a splendid way of buying other companies, their profits, assets, and potential on the cheap. Bid with cash, and it could cost 15pc or more in interest charges on the cash. Use high-flying shares, and the effective cost could be as low as the dividend yield on those shares – perhaps 2pc. Once issued, though, shares are forever. Dividends have to be paid on them, year in, year out. And profits must be earned to pay those dividends. Bank borrowings can always be repaid to save interest charges. Only rarely do companies repurchase any significant quantity of their own shares and trim dividend charges.

Nonetheless, acquisitions by share issue are popular, especially when the market is good. Banks like to see companies with a large slug of risk capital in relation to borrowings. The theory is that when times get tough, companies can cut dividends to save money, so the interest paid to the banks is that much safer. Ordinary share capital is risk capital, so banks are happy to see companies expand their risk capital base. That, in turn, allows the companies to borrow more from the banks. It is all about gearing, that sort of thing. When times are good, everybody is happy.

The pluses and minuses are complex, but when a share is running, few pause to argue. For budding entrepreneurs building growth companies, the main problem can be ensuring that they do not issue too many shares, and leave themselves with too small a slice of the cake they are baking.

Growth stocks are wonderful when the market is rising. Beautiful profits keep coming through, and a flow of deals makes it difficult for sceptics to analyse things too closely. The element of sustainable, organic growth can be difficult to split from the one-off profits, and the clever accounting tricks. As profits mount, so the shares are pushed up, and opportunities for yet more profitable deals emerge. For a while, it looks like a machine for perpetual motion, and everlasting share trading profits.

Watch out. Growth stocks can be forgiven one hiccup, provided the excuses are plausible. Two hiccups, though, can be fatal to the rating, and the game stops.

Always remember that few stocks grow for ever. The bigger they get, the tougher it is to keep up the pace. Hanson illustrates that point vividly.Deals need to be ever larger to make any real impact. Always stand by the door, ready to make your excuses and leave with a profit. Do not hesitate. Do it the minute you start to feel uneasy. If you are getting that itch, how many other investors will be feeling it too? First one out is the winner.

RECOVERY STOCKS

Recovery stocks are simply super – provided they recover. You find them when the hard times are almost over, in industries which have fallen from favour. Housebuilders, metal bashers, and electronics seem to be perpetual favourites, but in the early nineties the list could go on much longer – garages, estate agents, stores, banks and so on. Sometimes, you come across the odd exception, a company in a growth industry that has fallen on bad times for exceptional reasons. Unfortunately, it is easy to wade into a depressed company, only to discover that it has further to fall, or that it takes ages to recover.

You can trawl around to find suitable candidates for recovery either by choosing particular industries which you reckon are due to get better, and then picking individual shares, or by finding a bombed-out share you fancy and trying to work out whether it is in the sort of business which will pick up. Do whatever suits you. Either way makes sense. On the whole, it will be harder to find a real recovery prospect unless it is in the sort of business which is plainly doing better – and in any boom industry, there are always a few laggards. In the early nineties, there is certainly no shortage of industries with ample room for a rebound. It should not be too hard to find them. So picking the individual companies could make the difference between average and special performance.

Look for signs of firm management. Tough though it may be on the workers, factory closures and redundancies can be good news for investors. Sales of subsidiary companies, assets outside the mainstream of the business, are also useful pluses. Swift surgery and concentration of effort can work wonders in reviving profits. It can bring several benefits. It cuts overheads and reduces general costs, may put an end to a loss-maker which was bleeding the business, and could produce a cash injection from any assets which are sold. The talk of companies emerging leaner and fitter at the end of difficult times is right. They have been forced to look carefully at costs, and cut them to the bone. When orders pick up, that means a greater proportion of revenue flows through to profit.

Companies which have been trimming back often find there is a bonus in the pension fund. Thanks to the dreadful Robert Maxwell, this has become a hot potato. But when a work-force is reduced, surpluses tend to accumulate in the pension fund. It can be perfectly legal and proper for the company to take some benefit from this. Clearly, any company has an obligation to be fair to pensioners and employees who are still contributing to the fund. Pensions should be raised and worker benefits enhanced. But in many cases, there is still a handsome surplus which may allow the company to reduce its own contributions. In no way would I condone clawing back cash from a fund. But slimmed-down businesses often find that they can take a pension holiday, not paying into the fund, for a few years. And that can be of great benefit to profits – something would-be investors should consider.

Management changes can be vital. They are engineered sometimes by the big investors, using their voting power behind the scenes to force changes of direction or actual changes in top management personnel. For my money, the big boys exercise that power too infrequently, allowing too many dud managers to linger on – and then take enormous golden handshakes when they finally do go.

Watch for big pay-offs especially. Rewarding failure may be upsetting, but when it happens, there is normally a good reason for it. The institutions will not have taken such a step unless they are convinced it is necessary. They will expect to see their efforts rewarded by much better future performance. And there is evidence that the institutions are becoming more alive to their responsibilities, forcing more movement.

So watch for board changes. The newspapers spotlight the more significant ones. Sometimes the old team simply decides to go, selling quietly to new boys who fancy their chances of rebuilding the business. That can be particularly rewarding.

Changes at the top often pep the share price. They make a good each-way bet. Either the new team succeeds, or a bidder steps in. The changes put pressure on the company, and the new managers find they are working under the threat of a takeover if they should fail. After a few months in the hot seat, the new boys usually trot around the City, keen to say what a good job they can do, begging big shareholders not to become impatient, and explaining a new strategy. That, too, can help the shares.

Always, though, pay special attention to assets at any would-be recovery stock. If there is no recovery, the assets will count. If the company goes bust, they will determine whether anything is left for shareholders ('No' is almost invariably the answer). The assets will allow new managers to rebuild the business, or attract a bidder. Avoid companies with heavy borrowings, umless there are parts which can be sold to cut debt.

PENNY STOCKS

Once upon a time, penny stocks were what the name suggests – shares selling for a few pence. Now, anything under 100p is liable to be called a penny stock. A whole industry grew up around them in the mid-eighties, with tip sheets and a unit trust. I wrote a book *How To Make A Killing in Penny Shares* to advise those who concentrated on this very special sector.

Things are not what they used to be in the penny share game. The unit trust has faded away, the tip sheets have seen falling sales, and quite a few penny share companies have gone bust. Many have left their fans nursing heavy losses. And in the early nineties, there are many more companies back in the old-style penny groove, with share prices down to 10p or less.

It is just be a matter of time before the excitement starts again. Once the boom gets under way, the penny stock sector will be the hot one to be in. There are bargains enough to be had there. Many low-priced companies were poor performers in the late eighties and the early nineties. But lots of good ones were dragged down with the dross.

Penny shares are appealing because they appear to give you more for your money. Buying 5,000 shares for 10p each seems much better than spending the same £500 on 100 shares at £5 each.

There are snags, of course. The dealing spread – the difference between the price you pay and the price you get when you sell – is fatter, and works against you. Shares with a middle price of £5 might well be 495p to sell, 505p to buy – a spread of 10p, or 2pc. The 10p shares might well be 9p to sell, 11p to buy – a spread of 2p, or 20pc. Your penny stock has to work much harder before you clear dealing costs and make a profit.

It is not all bad. When a penny share moves, it moves much faster than a heavier-priced rival, because it takes proportionately bigger strides. On a 10p share, the next middle price up will be 10½p, a theoretical 5pc gain (though still a long way from making money). The £4 share may have moved up to 505p, a gain of 1pc. When a share is sliding, a penny stock seems to race away from you. A fall from 10p to 9½p middle price means that the shares which may have cost 11p will only fetch 8½p if you sell – a hefty loss with the first setback to the share price.

All the while, the investment fundamentals remain the same for a penny stock as for a heavyweight. A share selling at 10p is theoretically worth the same as one selling at £5 if they are both on a price earnings ratio of 20, and a dividend yield of 2pc.

The lesson comes home clearly when there is a scrip issue or a share split. If your £5 share had a nominal value originally of £1, and the board decided to split each £1 nominal share into ten shares of 10p nominal value, the price would then fall to 50p for each share – but since there would then be ten of them for every one held previously, there would be no real change in the value of the company. Suddenly, though, the £5 share is a 50p penny share.

There is merit in the argument that penny shares have more roon to grow than the big boys. It is a little deceptive, in truth, a bit of a cheat. Though it is generally applied to penny stocks, it should more accurately be used on small companies. It fits usually because penny stocks tend to be smallish companies.

Look at ICI. That is unlikely to grow ten-fold over the next decade. A low-priced, penny stock company just might. It might more easily go bust, too. Penny share fans are really saying that they have found a gambling counter which might take off, and are backing that instead of some big, established company in a more mature stage of development, with much lower risk. The old maxim – high risk, high reward – creeps back again.

That is not to knock penny shares. I am a firm fan. They can be terrific fun, and wonderfully rewarding. But many are in small, highly speculative companies. Just be sure you understand that.

Their main attraction, in the end, comes back to the psychological factor – they simply feel cheaper. Laughable in theory, this is important in practice. Tip sheets and more speculative stockbrokers are always keen to follow low-priced shares. They know they will find more takers for them among private clients than for the heavyweights. The more takers, the higher the share price will rise.

Penny shares slumped dramatically in the Crash of '87, often shedding half of their value quickly, and then drifting still lower. Unlike some of the leaders, which also tumbled heavily, some penny shares still ended that year with a good profit. Because they had risen so far, they had plenty of room to fall, and still come out ahead. The long, slow grind in 1988, 1989, 1990 and 1991 gradually took its toll of the brightest winners, however. It became hard to sell them in any decent quantity, and the prices dribbled ever lower.

Nonetheless, the eighties brought a whole new breed of penny share punters. They are still out there, waiting for the right conditions to try again, beginning to stir early in 1992. Never have I subscribed to the City chat about the small punters being fools who always rush in at the top. Many wait, staying out of the market until they are reasonably sure that they have a fair chance of winning. Penny shares will be there, providing fun and profits galore, in the stock market boom which is brewing in the nineties.

CHAPTER NINE
THE SHELL GAME

Five times a night or not, company directors are only human. They are in the great stock market game for much the same reasons as you are – the fun and the money. They only begin to tune in to the notion of a knighthood, building a business for posterity, the good of the nation and all that other ego-boosting stuff in their later years. Having fun and making money amount to very nearly the same thing for most company directors. So long as they are making the money for their company and building a rising share price, then the interests of directors and investors coincide nicely. That is the angle to watch – the way the money goes.

Making money retains a fascination for company promoters long after it would satisfy the wildest dreams of most people. The first million matters because that is spending stuff, money to live on. The next however many tens of millions matter, too, because by then the promoters have been trapped by the game. Every extra pound is another point gained. The money itself may not matter, but the score certainly does. And if you have built up a thriving public company, you are concerned about playing the game – taking on all-comers, and beating them.

Brilliant money-making players pop up every so often at the head of a new issue, and we have already explored how to get a piece of the new issue action. Just as often, though, the real movers try their hand at shaking up an old company in the shell game. Spotting candidate companies for the shell game can be one of the most rewarding of all stock market moves.

Shells come in all shapes and sizes, generally the smaller the better. The idea is to take control of a company which is going nowhere much, pop an unquoted business in, and use it as a base on which to build. The companies going in will generally be too young or small to gain a quotation in their own right. Put a group of them together under bright management and you can build an exciting business fast – and highly profitably. Already, there is ample evidence that this technique has lost none of its allure in the nineties. Through 1991 and into 1992, new management teams with ambitious ideas were moving quietly into several small companies. Make no mistake. The fun has started already among the lads convinced that the share boom is on the way.

THE FIRST CLUES

Would-be shell promoters want a company where they can buy control, or perhaps a 29.9pc stake, as cheaply as possible. Profits may not be too important, but ideally the target company will have some assets, preferably cash, or something which can be turned into cash fairly easily – share stakes, a subsidiary or two which might be sold, perhaps property. Often the shell will have hit a poor trading patch under established directors who are getting long in the tooth and lack the heart for the wholesale reconstruction required to whip the business back into shape.

The new promoter may start quietly building a small share stake. Anything over 3pc has to be announced publicly. Who is to say, though, that a few friends – totally unconnected and unaware of any plan so far as the Takeover Code is concerned, you understand – may not pick up a small stake or two as well?

Step two is to try to get the board to sell a few more shares. Watch for announcements of stakes changing hands. Everyone keeps an eye out for them. and sometimes prices soar as soon as a new 3pc plus investor pops up. However, there is a risk in leaping in after a big rise. The new would-be hero may be blocked by the board, or unable to buy more shares without the price running too far ahead. In some cases, it may all be a bluff. Someone might pick a stake and make their presence felt in the hope of pushing the price up and making a quick and profitable sale. Sometimes, the lack of a price surge after news of a stake may be disturbing. It may mean the market men know nothing much is going to happen. Or you might just have spotted one that they have missed. Try to make doubly sure. Usually, however, the patient investor will come to little harm by seeing the professionals move in first, even if it means paying a shade more. Look upon it as an insurance policy.

The next big step comes when the new promoter moves in publicly. This will involve either buying shares from the board and making a bid for the rest, or selling a company to the quoted one in return for sufficient shares to yield control. Either option is promising. If there is a full cash bid, it will usually be way below the share price, and holders will not be expected to take it. Under Takeover Panel rules, such a bid has to be made by anyone with more than 29.9pc. If it comes, check who is underwriting it – providing the cash. That will give a clue to the muscle behind the new promoter.

If a company is being sold in, watch who is providing the professional advice – the bankers, stockbrokers, and auditors. The bigger the names, the better. Check, too, if they are staying on as advisers. The right names will be more acceptable to the City in future deals, and it is important to get them involved as early as possible.

In some cases, you will find that the new promoter is going to end up with 29.9pc or less of the shell. That will mean that no bid is intended, and either the target company is too big for the newcomer to bid for fully, or perhaps further share issues will follow in time. Either way, the action will be starting.

READING THE PLANS

Obviously it is worth watching for anything the new team has to say. The type of company being sold in will usually indicate the intended area of expansion. At this stage, it does not greatly matter what is offered for public consumption. You really only need clear assurances that expansion is on the menu. Organic growth (growth from within a company) is fine for established operators, but you want newcomers to make it clear they are planning to grow by buying businesses. It is quicker that way. Stock Exchange rules sometimes make it difficult to signal the real plan. Companies are supposed to stay in the same line of business, and any radical change may need to be made in stages. Any big deal must be approached slowly. Minnows are not allowed to swallow whales without a mass of red tape, so small fish have to be fattened carefully before the big bite, for fear of frightening the authorities.

No matter how implausible the official story, the mere arrival of someone new will be enough to generate interest. Players rarely get beyond stage one without lining up well-informed support for the next stage. As usual, the insiders know best. It may not mean that all shareholders are given equal access to information, but insiders have their uses – and the money to back promising newcomers who may have big ideas.

What you want is a hungry newcomer, keen to make his fortune by buying businesses. Unfortunately, hungry newcomers are not allowed to advertise their intentions too openly in documents to shareholders, but they can give a few clues.

SPOTTING THE HUNGRY YOUNG MEN

Look hard at any potted career history in company documents, and note the age of the new chief executive. Under 28 is suspect – he may be too flash, too inexperienced, and out to make a quick buck at any price. Over 52 may simply be over the hill, and have left it too late to make real money in the game, unless he is a veteran who has played it successfully in the past – or comes in alongside bright, younger talent. Ideally, you want someone with a measure of experience, and time, ambition and energy enough to build something big – a hungry young man. If he has worked with major companies, or at the feet of the previous generation of company promoters, he might be just right – and could bring valuable support from his old associate – covertly or quite openly.

Beware of anyone linked to previous duds. In this game, it rarely pays to give a loser a second chance.

Most important, see how the new player and his team take their share stake. Watch what they have paid, either by buying shares or the value put on shares they are taking in exchange for anything they are pumping in. Check, too, whether there are restrictions on when they can sell their shares, and if they have options to take more, perhaps linked to profit targets. Check what prices they will pay, and when they will get their extra shares.

Comb the fine print at the back of the document, looking through the material contracts to see if they have done other deals for shares. Work out the price they have paid. And scan their contracts of employment to see whether they are on a slice of profits. The deeper they are committed, the harder they will work.

Price points or profit targets when they take more shares will give you the best glimpse of what is expected, how they see the company developing. You can bet they have not set targets they do not think they can reach. It may take extra application, but it is worth sitting down with a calculator and working out the detail of what it all could mean to them. Do not take the percentages and multiples on trust, and guess whether they look generous. Do the arithmetic. It can be quite staggering. Sometimes you will be astonished just how large a take the new team may plan, if they achieve their top targets. Through the years, I have been horrified how few shareholders – large or small – actually bother. The answers can be breath-taking – though as a new shareholder you may want to applaud the greed, not complain. Just so long as there is enough gravy left for the outside shareholders as well.

DANGER SIGNALS

In a rising market, the honeymoon will normally last about six months, or until the first sizeable deal – whichever comes first. If nothing has happened after six months, beware. Something is wrong. Sell, unless you can establish very sound reasons for staying on.

Now and then, a promising shell is used to float smallish companies dominated by family directors with little experience outside their own business. Tread carefully. That kind of deal will set the family up nicely, and rakes in fat fees for the original finders of the shell and those who got in before the action started. However, there may be no great follow-through, as the family sit with the prestige of a public company, selling shares from time to time and watching their business grow quietly, without plans for dynamic growth.

RECONSTRUCTIONS

Managed carefully, a successful shell can be built into a stock market monster. Profits from picking the right one and sticking with it can be enormous. Polly Peck may be the most spectacular example of recent times. That came unstuck after nine glorious years. But Greg Hutchings, who learnt his trade with Hanson, has done brilliantly at F.H. Tomkins. And Nigel Rudd and Brian McGowan have built Williams Holdings into a first-class company. There are many others. Still more came unstuck in the recession, but yielded enormous profits for those who backed them on the way up. And that is all that need concern you – hitching a ride up. What you want is a share trading profit, not part of a monument to endure for ever. HIT AND RUN.

Purists might argue over definitions. Some big winners might appear more like reconstructions than shells. But the principles are the same – spot a modest business which is not going anywhere, reshape it and pump in new companies to generate growth. The reconstruction may be a little harder to spot because the chosen company might not appear such an obvious case for treatment, and the first deal might not be particularly attractive. But such companies are well worth seeking, whatever you call them.

FUND-RAISING

Definitions are for dictionaries. They do not matter to the share trader. What you want is action, in a shell or a reconstructed company. Either way, if you miss the first stages, you may be able to clamber aboard when the first major fund-raising exercise is launched. Most new boys with big ideas will soon want more cash. It makes life easier in a myriad of ways. The popular method of getting it is by a rights issue – offering new shares to existing investors at a special price.

This expands the capital base, widening the scope for bank and other borrowings. It also allows the promoter, or his backers, to raise their share stake on the cheap. The price of the rights will usually be pitched well below the market price, but well above the real worth of the business. It is a classic means of using the market, translating hope into hard cash, which can then be employed – if all goes well – to justify that hope, and generate a still fatter premium for still more hope.

The impact of a fund-raising move depends on the state of the market. It might well be timed to accompany a kitchen sink exercise. Unless the market is in good shape, and well attuned to what is happening, it might knock the price a bit, and create a real buying opportunity.

The kitchen sink exercise is a time-honoured ritual. The new management goes in, looks around, clucks, and decides that things were really much worse than expected. So they take an axe to everything in sight. Assets are written down, stock values chopped, provisions are set aside for redundancy and reorganisation, and the grimmest view possible is attached to previous trading. Perhaps employing new auditors, anything which might be taken as a loss is thrown in. The published figures are absolutely dreadful, and the new managers sit smiling, hand on heart, saying they have taken the responsible view, and had a real accounting clear-out, tossing out all of the old management's skeletons.

As a public relations move, it is sound. It makes a virtue out of necessity, and perhaps creates a wonderful opportunity for further advancement. Tucked away in the accounting clear-out will be the kind of tough treatment which may overstate the damage, leaving room for some losses to be written back quietly into profits in the future. That flatters the new boy, gives him time to breathe, extra scope for looking good. And it may persuade Stock Exchange officials and others that the new share issue price should not be pitched too high, or make a few unsophisticated investors feel things are really so bad that it is not worth supporting. That way, some shareholders will not take up their rights, leaving the new team to buy them as underwriters. Either way, the home team gets a good chunk of extra stock at a bargain rate – though only they know how much of a bargain.

WATCH THE WAY THE MONEY FLOWS. If the new team is putting more cash in, that means more than anything they say. Words are cheap, cash is precious. They are out to make money for themselves first, their chums second, and their advisers next. Shareholders are there to be used. But if they stay awake, they can do very nicely, too. It does not always work quite that way. Fund-raising may send the price up at first, if the market is roaring. Then it will tend to sit quietly for a spell, awaiting the next move. That is the time to buy. If you got in early, always take up your rights if you can. Fund-raising is the surest of all signs that the new team is serious, and set for action. THEY WILL NOT BE PUTTING MONEY IN UNLESS THEY EXPECT TO MAKE A PROFIT ON IT.

THE PUBLIC RELATIONS PUSH

As the first big fund-raising hits, it should begin to attract attention in the City pages. This will be an encouraging sign that the insiders are playing the game. City public relations firms galore are employed to see that the press gets the latest company announcements and documents. The agencies vary from sophisticated postmen to outright share pushers who cultivate journalists with a view to persuading them to be nice about their clients. The idea is to create a good, positive image, and discourage adverse comment. They push out gossip which ranges from solid insider information to wild dreams based on pure invention.

Used sensibly, public relations can help everyone. Inevitably, it goes over the top at times, and one or two public relations agents become the kiss of death, pushing losers or short term spiv operators.

The outside investor may be unaware of this. Watch, though, for repeated mentions in market reports, where it is easier to place uncritical plugs. At one stage before Blue Arrow went wrong, chief executive Tony Berry seemed to appear there almost every day. George Walker, the Brent Walker boss, was another favourite with market reporters. Keep a critical eye open. Too many puffs supported by little substance may suggest the wrong kind of p r push. What you want is the more analytical journalists backing up the chat with careful reasoning, firmer projections of profits. And where newspapers carry stockbroker tips, you want to see 'buy' recommendations from the better-established broking houses.

All such comments, of course, should be put firmly in context. If you are chasing quick profits in a frothy market, you may be delighted by any puffery, and happy to ride on it. Good enough. But, once again, be under no illusions. If you are playing the short-term game, be ready to sell on the first setback.

WHAT YOU WANT TO SEE

Once aboard, stay for the ride so long as it feels good. What you want to see are;
*   an increase in earnings per share with each deal
*   each deal generating cash, via the company which is being bought, or through selling assets, or through other fund-raising
*   rising dividends
*   directors raising their share stake by new purchases or options
*   a price earnings ratio which holds above the average
*   a stable core of top managers
*   a stable set of top City advisers
*   sizeable share stakes spread among big City investors
*   at least one significant deal every nine months
*   projections of rising profits in 'buy' notes from stockbrokers
*   the name of the chief executive or chairman attracting sensible press comment.

WHAT YOU DO NOT WANT

Investment fashions change. The economy may turn down, or your superstar promoter could stumble, so watch for the danger signs. The things you do not want are almost a mirror image of the positive signs listed above. You do not want;

*   deals which cut earnings per share

*   increasing debt

*   higher stocks and work in progress

*   large share sales by the board

*   static dividends

*   a price earnings ratio down to a single figure

*   constant management changes

*   changes in City advisers

*   long periods without expansion news

*   innovative ways of raising cash by new-fangled pieces of paper

*   the top man joining other boards, taking a seat on Government bodies, the CBI, or City authorities

*   directors telling the press the shares are cheap

*   a move to new headquarters in Mayfair or Docklands

*   talk of going into financial services

*   the top man winning any award as something or other of the year.

Tread carefully, too, once the market capitalisation exceeds £500 million. By then it may be more difficult to find suitable targets to buy. Tread even more gently when the capitalisation goes over £1bn. The company may still prosper, but the shares are much less likely to double or treble in a year. They may still do nicely, but the earlier excitement will have faded. Early fans may be taking profits, many big investors will already have shares enough, and future growth may involve issuing lots of shares in an unwelcome takeover which could attract damaging comment from the target company. If you stay with the shares, you might be best advised to take some profits. This may no longer be the go-go stock you bought originally.

MORE WARNING SIGNALS

Everyone has their own danger signs. Bill Mackey was a partner in top accountants Ernst &

Whinney, and the man apppointed receiver to countless company collapses, public and private. His warning signals may appear to be tongue in cheek, but they are well worth heeding nonetheless. Down the years, they have proved remarkably prescient. He frowned at;

* directors driving Rolls-Royces with personalised number plates
* a fountain in the reception area
* a flagpole outside the factory
* the Queen's Award for Industry – UK only
* the chairman honoured for services to industry
* new offices opened by the Prime Minister
* an unqualified or elderly accountant (a real killer that one)
* products which are market leaders
* 'Hi-tech' in the company name
* an audit partner who grew up with the company
* a politician well known for public works as chairman
* satisfied personnel with no strike record
* a recently announced technological break-through
* whiz-kid chairman
* winners of The Accountant award for the best report and accounts
* a picture in the accounts of the chairman getting out of a helicopter
* an office in China.

YET MORE DANGER SIGNS

In the early nineties, we might substitute a Bentley Turbo for the Rolls-Royce in Bill Mackey's list. What should we add?

* a staff magazine with more than two pictures of the chairman
* report and accounts too large or strange to fit normal filing cabinets
* soft focus colour pictures of the board behind semi-transparent protective sheets
* shareholder meetings close to Christmas or New Year's Eve, at 10 in the morning or on Friday afternoon

* shareholder meetings closed to the press

* directors who do not appear or answer questions at annual meetings

* the chairman's yacht

* chairman or chief executive on the board of a football club

* the chairman or chief executive in the Nigel Dempster column

* any director who plays polo

* any director who claims to play polo with, or be a friend of the Prince of Wales.

CHAPTER TEN
THE BID BONANZA

Gone are the days when a takeover bid was a major event. Nowadays they are commonplace, and no company can consider itself safe. Some of the most famous names in British industry have succumbed – tobacco giant Imperial Group, Scotch whisky aristocrat Distillers, performance car builder Jaguar, and High Street chains like Currys, Debenhams, and British Home Stores. The early nineties might not have been so frantic as the mid eighties, when rumours swirled around almost any company you could think of. But the fun will start again as the market gathers steam.

If you are a share trader, forget the debate about whether bids are good for Britain, good for industry, or serve the consumer well. While the system lasts, what matters to the active investor is the chance of fat, quick profits. A bid is the great bonus, a short-cut to capital gains which might have taken years if left to profits growth alone. Never mind industrial strategy – enjoy the soaring share price.

That bid-and-damn it philosophy applies all across the City, no matter what the mouth-pieces may pretend. Bankers and brokers have departments combing company records, looking for suitable bid targets, companies they can help break up, sell, float, or manipulate in some way. The whole thing is fee-driven. They have vastly expensive offices and staff desperate to earn money advising companies. So they must generate corporate action. All of the top merchant banks and brokers – and especially the aggressive Americans – regularly circulate schemes suggesting one company might take on another, or how established companies might be broken up, complete with computations of how profitable it might be to the management. So the big boys are working for you, doing all they can to stimulate bids. Poor dears, they need the money.

Some of the most beautiful shares on the market belong to growing companies which have bid prospects thrown in. Choose carefully, and you have a triple winner – a share which rises because trading is good and profits are rising, a share which bobs higher on rumours of a bid, and – Oh happy day – a share which leaps when a bid actually appears.

SPOTTING A BID STOCK

Finding such a stock can be hard, but not impossible. There are clues a'plenty. Unfortunately, there are no guarantees. Some stocks remain bid stocks for 20 years or more, always the bridesmaid and never the bride. It would be tempting fate to mention the names here. The faithful cling to them still, convinced that the offer will have arrived by the time you read this – or pretty soon, anyway.

The ideal bid stock will have a good profits record, heavy asset backing, a fair spread of investors without large blocks of stock stuck in the hands of a small number of long-term holders, and a slice of a growing section of industry. That is pretty near the ideal stock, let alone a bid stock. Find any two of those qualities, and you could be in with a fair chance.

PROFIT MARGINS

Look, too, for established names which have gone off the boil. Profit margins may be important here. You can do simple margin sums by dividing pre-tax profits into sales or turnover. If other companies in the same line of business are making fatter margins, ask yourself why. Your company might be inefficient, or there might be one or two bad bits making losses, or tiny returns, tucked away among the good. Either way, unless they are in shrinking industries, they could attract a livelier competitor who might want to buy the turnover to boost margins (and profits) to his own level. Or perhaps simply to close down and sell the loss-makers.

CAPITAL RETURNS

Returns on capital are trickier. Retailers are fond of checking how much trading space their rivals own, and calculating sales per square foot. If they themselves get a higher return, they may be interested in bidding. That kind of reasoning sparked the Burton bid for the Debenhams department stores, and the Dixons bid for Currys. Others look at brand names, which are often in the balance sheet at a low figure. They calculate their worth under different management, with more attention to maximising profits, or perhaps with greater investment in new products under established names. Most companies have spotted this one. There has been keen debate about the correct way of valuing brands. Some companies have slapped high figures in their balance sheet for what are, essentially, intangible assets. It makes sense for some companies – and is a downright liberty for others.

TIRED FAMILIES

Families who have controlled a company for years and lost their motivation or touch are fair game for bidders. Sometimes the younger generation does not follow their parents into the business, and the original directors opt out and seek a bidder so they can slip quietly into retirement. It is hard, however, to distinguish between large holders who are determined to hang on, and those ready to go.

BOMB-BLASTED BUSINESSES

Bomb-blasted businesses are really our old friends, recovery stocks, in a slightly different guise. A bad year or two may have shattered the share price, and the management may lack the nerve or verve to put the business back together again. Look for companies which have grown fat with assets, have over-expanded, or are bowed down by loss-makers and heavy borrowings. There may be opportunities for selling either good businesses to slash borrowings, or bad ones to eliminate losses. If borrowings come down, the interest burden can be lifted, and profits may leap.

SHARE STAKES

Many bidders telegraph their intentions by picking up a share stake before they actually bid. It is not completely daft. Sometimes it destabilises the shareholder list, and puts a company in play. Speculative buyers pick up blocks of shares, and are more ready to sell to a bidder, making it harder for the company to defend itself. Watch the City pages for news of stakes. They will spark a flurry of interest and the price will rise. If the company looks right, go in then. It might be our old friend, the shell promoter. Or it could be a fully-fledged bidder. The bidder might sit for a few months, allowing the price to settle back, and you might be able to buy more cheaply on a dull day. They always come, sooner or later.

Try for shares in companies with price earnings ratios around the average for their sector, with reasonable trading prospects. That way, you might be able to ride the bid roundabout without an additional entry fee. Even if the first stakeholder does not bid, there is always the chance he will sell to another bidder. Once a stake has been announced, there are always chances – if no bid appears, you will get periodic bursts of action as the market speculates that something is about to happen. The fly boys may be stuck, and they are expert at generating rumours so they can scramble out.

LEAKS

In theory, bids should come like bolt from the blue. In practice, illegal or not, insiders get to work in four bids out of five, and nibble at the shares. The press, especially the market reports, gives the best guide. Watch, too, for shares which keep edging to new highs or hold steady on days when all about them are falling. Someone knows something.

Study comments which are reported in response to bid rumours. A flat 'No comment' is pretty impenetrable, but it is astonishing how often company representatives give a clue, unwittingly or not. Any reservation at all can be the sign of an honest person who cannot admit what is afoot but will not offer a bare-faced lie. Even so, bare-faced lies do pop out from time to time. That is part of the reason for employing public relations agents. They parrot what they are told. It can be dismissed later by the company as a mistake, or a misunderstanding. So the most vehement denial may not be the end of the story. It may be a deliberate attempt to mislead, or it may even be that the press is ahead of the game, and the company itself has not yet learnt of the bid which is on its way.

You are on dangerous ground, though, buying bid stocks on leaks from friends in the business. If your source knows for sure, it is illegal to tell you, and illegal for you to act on the tip. If your source does not know for sure, you could be buying shares which are being run up by market men spreading the story so that they can sell. You could be buying a pup.

WHAT TO DO WHEN THE BID COMES

If you have shares when a bid comes, hallelujah. Life is suddenly bright and beautiful. Sit back and enjoy it. You may be bombarded with circulars, but the more the merrier. The more attention you receive, the higher the final bid is likely to be. Until the closing stages, all you need worry about is the Monopolies Commission. These days, most bidders seek quiet guidance first, and do not move unless they know that they are likely to escape a reference to the Commission. The system is not infallible, however, and some bids do get referred. If a reference seems likely, sell straight away. It can mean a six month delay, or, more likely, will prompt the bidder to walk away. Otherwise do nothing until the last possible moment.

The waiting game is the winning game in a bid. Make your decision just before the very last closing date, never by the first. Once a bidder has sent an offer document to shareholders, they have 60 days. If they have not won by then, they cannot try again for a year. Nowadays, though, counter-bidding and general jiggery-pokery introduce all manner of complexities, and bids can drag on for months and months. The first bid is rarely the highest, and the first bidder may not be the winning bidder.

You should act eventually, however. Do not let a bid slip by without doing something – unless, of course, it is for shares in the kind of shell company we touched on earlier. Those sort of bid shares you must keep.

If they choose, successful bidders can force you to take their bid once acceptances are over 90pc of the share capital for which the offer was made. Watch this. By then you may have no option but to take the shares they are offering. Any cash alternative, if there was one, may have closed earlier.

TAKING THE CASH BID

Your tax position will probably be the most important factor in deciding whether to take cash or shares. Once you take cash, you have effectively sold as far as the tax man is concerned, so you may have incurred a capital gains tax liability. This will only matter if your total gains in that tax year are above the annual free allowance. Before you choose cash, check the market price. The value of the bidder's paper (shares) offer may have pushed your shares above the cash alternative, so you might do better selling in the market.

ACCEPTING SHARES

If you accept shares in a bid, you defer your liability to capital gains tax until you sell those shares. This can be a big advantage. You need to be sure, however, that the shares are worth keeping. Look to see what price the cash alternative puts on them (effectively the price the bidder's shares are being underwritten at). This gives you an idea of what the institutions think the shares are worth. They will not want to see them below that.

Check, too, what your income will be if you take shares. Many bids incorporate fixed interest stock as part of the bid currency. That is done to make sure that shareholders do not end up with a lower dividend income by accepting. If income is what you want, you might do better taking the cash, and re-investing in other high yielders. Bear in mind that if you take part fixed interest capital and part Ordinary shares, you will have two lots of dealing expenses if you sell later.

TURNING DOWN A BID

At times, you might think it worth turning down a bid. Most shareholders feel a certain allegiance to their directors, and take more notice of them than of the bidder. The defending board will produce a flurry of promises which the City will expect them to keep. Usually, shares in a company which has fought off a bid fall when the offer lapses. But if the board has put up a strong enough case, they might attract a permanently higher rating. In many cases, the original bidder, or perhaps another, pops up again. Obviously, if the losing bidder has accumulated a sizeable share stake, further action is likely eventually.

BUYING WHEN A BID ARRIVES

No matter how dedicated a detective you might be, you cannot spot bid stocks to order. Do not despair. If you have the nerve – and usually you do not need much of it – you can still do well buying after the bid arrives. This became increasingly popular in the mid eighties as merger mania gripped the market. It was fuelled by events in America, where people like Sir James Goldsmith bought blocks of stock in companies, then were paid extra to go away. Ivan Boesky made a remarkable reputation as an arbitrageur, making massive profits by buying shares after the first bid appeared. Later, of course, he was exposed as a cheat and insider. But the message struck home – the first bid is rarely the final, highest bid. Buy when an offer first appears, and you could still do nicely.

The financial muscle of the US arbitrageurs allowed them to help shape events. The small investor cannot do that, but there is ample scope for profit. The chances of losing are modest, if you are careful not to pay too much over the original offer price. At least you are assured of action.

WHAT BID LANGUAGE REALLY MEANS

Obviously an agreed bid is no use to you. There is no reason for the shares to rise above the offer, no chance of making more. Most bids, though, are disputed, and the more bitterly, the better. So you need to read between the lines when the combatants start talking.

Under the rules of the Takeover Panel, bidders are not allowed to describe their offer as 'final' until near the very end. Before then, there is always the chance that they will pay more, no matter how much they huff and puff. There is an almost automatic assumption that the first bid is a sighting shot, meant to draw the defence and to measure more accurately what it might really take to win. So disregard what the bidder may say, until the offer is final.

Almost any bid which is not agreed at the very beginning will turn into a battle. The first statement from the target company will give an important clue to their attitude. If it follows almost immediately after the terms of the offer, and talks of inadequate, unsuitable terms, they are planning a tough fight. If the first response takes a day or two, or simply advises shareholders to do nothing for the moment, that also means a fight is on, but perhaps the defender is not in quite so strong a position – they need to think carefully before blasting off. The routine has become much more familiar, however, and some of the craftier players now simply take extra time to think before saying anything.

As ever, the press is a crucial source of information. Look for signs that the two sides have had preliminary talks. If they had, and the bidder is going ahead without agreement, the fight could be really bitter. The two sides have already established that they cannot get on. Watch, too, for any hint of another bidder, or a white knight – a friendly counter-bidder.

Try to judge the emphasis on independence, and whether there could be readiness to sell to someone other than the first bidder. Check whether the bidder has a share stake, or if there are other stakeholders who might enter the fray. Watch how many shares defending directors control, and whether they really count. Particular institutions have a habit of supporting boards – Britannic Assurance (strong in Midlands engineering companies), and unit trust group M & G are especially prominent. The more shares which look like backing the board, the more likely the bidder will have to pay extra.

Directors have a natural inclination to fight for their jobs. That angle serves the interests of shareholders, provided it does not get out of hand. In the end, however, they have an obligation to take a good bid. The institutions recognise this. They themselves must work in the best interests of their shareholders and policyholders.

The victims most likely to put up a strong fight or attract another bid are the best quality companies. The fatter the asset backing, the bigger the bid. The better the profits record, the higher the worth of the company. Any bid should automatically offer a premium for control, so any company should expect to be taken out for at least 1½ times the average price earnings ratio for the sector.

THE BANKERS TO BACK

Last but by no means least in deciding bid strategy is the identity of the merchant banks and brokers involved. League tables change. In the mid eighties, Morgan Grenfell was top of the banking pops, thanks largely to the innovative and imaginative abilities of corporate finance man Roger Seelig. He ended up in court as a result of the Guinness affair, and Morgan's star waned. Hill Samuel was another to take a knock, this time from the Panel, in a bid defence. The whole bank ended up being taken over by the Trustee Savings Bank.

But you need a tough fighter, ready to go to the limit in a bid defence. Top names in the nineties include Warburg, Kleinwort Benson, Rothschild, Lazard Brothers, Schroder Wagg, Barings and County Natwest.

BUYING AFTER A WINNING BID

Should you buy shares of the winner after a winning bid? This works sometimes as the market realises what a good deal the bidder has got. And if you had shares in the company which was taken over and you took cash, it might be a good idea to buy into the victorious group if there is a slide in the price after the bid and you think your company went cheap. Usually, however, a winning bidder's shares slumber a while as the market absorbs the extra capital, and as the directors get down to sorting out their acquisition. Give it a few months, maybe three or four, then take a look.

If, however, your winning bidder is a shell company, or one being built quickly by ambitious new managers, the quiet spell after the bid may be the time to buy. Sooner or later, the next bid proposition will be lined up, and the bidder will need to get the share price motoring to help finance it. Around that time – what a coincidence – reports will start filtering out to big City investors, and through the company's brokers, recounting just what a wonderful deal the previous bid has proved to be. Pick a sufficiently aggressive company, and it can make sense to buy in the wake of a winning bid.

CHAPTER ELEVEN
THE STREETWISE SHARE TRADER

Learning about the stock market and share trading never stops. Commit every line, every comma, of this book to heart, and you will be on the way to making a killing in the share jungle. But there will still be much more to learn. The more you understand the theory, the better. There are guides galore to how things ought to work, but they are no substitute for experience and the personal touch which only you can add.

All along, I have tried to flesh out theory with insight into what really happens, tricks of the trade. Theories give a rough guide, the rules which work until someone spots a smarter way. They are valuable because they tell you roughly how everyone else will approach things. The crowd pushes shares up or down. You want to anticipate what the crowd will do, get there first, and take advantage of it – a blink ahead of the action.

You are taking on all-comers. When you do. it helps to become streetwise, alert to everything around you, alive to the impact of changing moods and the way everyday events influence companies and share prices. After a while, it becomes natural, instinctive. The streetwise share trader develops a feel for how people react, the way prices respond, how the more routine developments – and the most improbable events – can shift shares.

BACKING THE MAN

It takes no great genius to appreciate that backing the right man is a formula for successful investment. It has come up several times already in the book, especially when looking at shell companies and reconstructions. It matters just as much in big companies as small ones. Sir John Harvey-Jones had a radical impact on Imperial Chemical Industries. With his straggly hair, garish kipper ties and energetic, abrasive style, he showed that there was much in ICI which warranted change. It impressed the City no end, and sent the shares to new peaks. A few years after he had gone, people began questioning his achievements. Never mind. For the alert investor, who had ridden the rise and sold before the slump, Sir John had been a man to follow.

In the High Street, a similar picture developed, but in more flamboyant style. Sir Terence Conran at Storehouse, Sir Ralph Halpern at Burton Group, and George Davies at Next all revolutionised their companies. So did Gerald Ratner. While they were on top, the shares enjoyed massive gains. All but Gerald have now gone, and the strategies of all four look wildly over-ambitious with hindsight. The shares have slumped. But while they were hot, they were really hot.

The great long distance runners, of course, are Lord Hanson and Lord White at Hanson, and Lord Weinstock at GEC. They have lost their edge, perhaps because their creations have grown too big to move swiftly. In their heyday, they were all marvellous. Already, I have mentioned Greg Hutchings at F.H. Tomkins, and Nigel Rudd and Brian McGowan at Williams Holdings as leaders of the next generation of big business winners. There are many more, coming up behind.

In the early nineties, it has become fashionable to decry the efforts of individual entrepreneurs, attack one-man band businesses, and sing the praises of supervision by a strong board, with a split between the functions of chairman and chief executive, and ample squads of non-exective directors on hand. I have my doubts. This is a response to the many failures to hit the recession years. With a few exceptions, government by committee does not work so well. For the aggressive share player, the big winners are still most likely to come from companies associated with one strong, determined individual.

Almost every stock market winner is associated with a driving personality at the top. The earlier you spot them, the better. You can do well by a shrewd selection of big companies, but the real excitement is in small to medium situations which are getting up speed. Pick the right man in the right company, and you could see the price double or treble in the first year, and again in the second. You will not get that sort of performance from too many industrial giants – though you just might if you time it well as the coming share boom gets under way. Remember, though, that smaller companies and one-man bands do carry higher risks.

USING YOUR INSTINCTS

Sorting the prospective high flyer from the common or garden director is not easy. Follow your instincts. If what he says and does seems sensible, back him. If it does not, do not be persuaded. Instinct and common sense are great investment tools. Time and again, they prove to be the winners. No matter what others may say, if the new hero strikes you as a shifty character who rarely gives a straight answer, keep clear.

EVERY CON-MAN HAS TO HAVE A STORY, has to be able to persuade people to believe in him if he is going to be able to rip them off. This may sound unduly cynical, the sour reaction of a hard-bitten journalist. Perhaps it is. In almost 30 years of reporting financial affairs, I have met hundreds of company promoters who have come unstuck. They were either out to take shareholders for a ride, or simply incapable of delivering the delights they promised. Every one had a fan club. Every one appeared to know all of the answers. So they should. No investor on the outside can understand what is going on inside a company as well as the person in charge.

Often the promoters themselves believe what they are saying, as they are saying it. They have a shining self-belief, faith in themselves and their schemes, a conviction that somehow it will all work out. Step back and think about what they are saying. Sometimes the cracks appear very quickly. A few minutes spent analysing what they actually promise, in the quiet, on your own, can give you a very different view.

My scepticism is hard-earned. I have listened to the promises, and watched the problems break in their wake. Then I have read the letters from disillusioned investors who have lost their savings. It can be shattering. After a while, believing becomes the most difficult thing of all.

It would be quite wrong, though, to pretend that I get it right every time. Every so often, I get taken in, and find myself believing something which turns out to be fatally flawed. It happens, no matter how much I try to heed my own warning signs. There are other times when I realise that I have been unduly harsh about some scheme which is relatively well-founded. That is a mistake I make less frequently, the sort of mistake all of us must accept. Every time, err on the side of caution. It is no great loss if you miss the odd good thing. You lose nothing real, no cash. If you do back a dud, you will know what you have lost – real money.

The man to follow is the man you can believe in. You need someone with personality and a plan, someone who makes sense, someone ambitious and – above all – someone whose own fortune depends on the success of the company.

Time and again, it does come down to instinct. Never neglect it. Never let it be over-ruled by the idea that so many clever chaps in the City see it differently. If the so-called experts never got it wrong, there would never be any suspect schemes, never any company collapses or scandals. Never give the suspect the benefit of the doubt. No matter how glittering the prize, there will always be another.

THE ANNUAL MEETING

Once you have backed your high flyer and bought his shares, make an effort to meet him. The annual meeting is your best opportunity, though while a company is growing fast, there may be several extraordinary meetings for investors to approve deals. Try to go to one. The annual meeting especially is the one occasion each year when this budding captain of industry is answerable to you as a shareholder, one of the owners of the company.

You may be unsure about confronting some well-known name, a man of power and repute. Grit your teeth. He will be nervous, too. Company directors are used to telling others what to do, demanding answers to their questions. A shrewdly posed question at an annual meeting can catch them off guard. Many rehearse replies to all likely questions, with advisers quizzing them ahead of the meeting, especially if something controversial is on the agenda.

Do not be put off. Do not be rude. Be polite, but firm. Frame your question with a compliment. Listen to the answer. If it does not make sense, or avoids the question, do not hesitate to come back. All too often, shareholders are overcome by nerves, too shy to pick up obvious evasions. Do not let it happen to you. You deserve a proper reply. You have taken the trouble to buy the shares, and come to the meeting. You have every right to be treated politely and intelligently. If you are not, learn from it. Ask yourself if this is a man and a company you should trust with your money.

Make any question brief, clear, and to the point. It does not have to be clever. A simple query about progress may be enough. Anything sensible will make a mark, and the chances are that the chairman or some director will come to talk to you about it afterwards. Always stay behind at the end of a meeting and chat to as many directors as you can. It gives you an excellent chance of weighing up the people who are responsible for your investment. Most genuinely welcome your interest. If they do not treat you as you think they should, beware. They are fools, and badly-advised fools at that.

USING YOUR EYES AND EARS

Many companies use annual meetings to display their products and services. This can give a valuable impression of what is really going on, and can ensure that you know what the company really does. That will help day to day investment judgements. It is routine for streetwise share traders to be picking up investment information no matter what they are doing. You can stumble across share tips anywhere, at any time, if you are alert enough to appreciate them.

The transformation of stuffy old menswear group J. Hepworth into high-flying fashion chain Next happened in the High Street for all to see. Drab Hepworth shops closed, and the clean, trendy lines of Next replaced them. A casual glance at the fashion spreads in the papers confirmed that Next boss George Davies was impressing everyone. If you backed him at the beginning, you could have multiplied your money five-fold. Perhaps you were smart enough to spot it going off the rails, with too many stores, conflicting brands, and so on.

No-one need telling about Laura Ashley, of course, as her designs caught on everywhere. Record fans who noticed the Our Price shops or watched TV commercials could have picked a winner and sold out to a lucrative bid in the eighties. Less obviously, anyone shopping for food in the eighties might have wondered at the increasing emphasis on fresh fruit and vegetables in supermarkets, and realised that companies like Albert Fisher, Glass Glover, and Hunter Saphir were doing nicely out of it. In the early nineties, the trends were mostly the other way. Keeping your eyes open produced warnings galore. There was Ratners with the never-ending cut-price offers. There were stores with sale after sale, bank branches closing, house prices falling. On the bright side, it was more difficult. But the expanding chain of Dillons bookshops showed that Terry Maher was getting it right at Pentos. And the collapse of Harry Goodman's International Leisure Group cleared the way for a boom in newer, smaller tour operators like Airtours and Owners Abroad.

On a global scale, the Gulf War killed an already flagging tourist business, hammering groups like Forte with their central London hotels. British Airways suffered badly, too.

Share tips – to buy or sell – are all around. You simply need to notice them.

LISTENING TO THE GOSSIP

Gossip may come your way at your local, or from neighbours on the train. A friend of a friend said chaps from another company have been crawling all over the works, a new plant is being planned, or a massive order is on the way, or uncle was told by someone who works in the City that someone is planning a takeover – but don't pass it on.

Do not trust the tip. Try to check it, by all means. Careless talk costs money. Employees are rarely good at judging the impact of events, real or imaginary, on the shares in their own company. They may well be out of touch with the market, and have no idea what the City is expecting, or knows already. A big development might mean more jobs, and sound good to the workers, but might mean a cash-flow shortage in the company, or lower profits for a while.

Bid whispers might be right – who knows? More often than not, they are wrong. Anyone who really knows about a bid is breaking the law by passing the word on, if they expect someone to buy shares as a result. If the tip is right, the chances are that the City has already heard it. You could be Tail-End Charlie, the last mug buyer.

Perhaps the most significant exception is where information has been released to unions, or staff meetings. This should not go outside the plant or office, but it does. More often than not, it is advance warning of bad news, trouble or staff cutbacks. There was classic example early in 1992, when I heard that staff in the Ratners jewellery group were to be addressed by area managers. Christmas trading had been grim, and cuts were in the air. In the next trading session, the shares fell 20pc. Be careful. Best rely on your stockbroker for share gossip. Test whatever you hear on him. He will have some idea of whether what you hear makes sense, and whether it will matter to the share price.

DIRECTOR DEALING

It has become fashionable to watch the way directors trade their shares. Several services publish charts based on board-room trading, and attempt to analyse what this means for prices. Those services make some questionable judgements, but the information itself is interesting. Directors should have a better idea than most of how the company is doing. Their trading is more likely than not to get the trend right – but it is by no means infallible.

Directors and their families are not allowed to deal in the two months ahead of scheduled company announcements – the interim and preliminary profit statements. Nor when they know price sensitive news is on the way. So sometimes they are forced to buy or sell at inconvenient, inopportune moments. And the routine excuses of needing to sell to pay off overdrafts, meet family needs, other personal reasons can be quite genuine. Companies like BRI Information Services, 42, Hagley Road, Birmingham, B16 8PZ (021 452 1842) offer a useful monitoring service. It is followed in several newspapers. You can get the same information, sometimes slightly earlier, from the Stock Exchange Weekly Official Intelligence in larger libraries.

WHAT THE CHAIRMAN REALLY MEANS

There is something about running a public company that brings out the pomposity in people. Even the most down to earth directors can get a touch pretentious when they write to shareholders in the name of the company. The words get in the way of what they mean to say.

It is not made any easier by a bewildering array of Stock Exchange, Takeover Panel, Companies Act, and Financial Services Act obstacles. Sometimes, it seems, merely opening your mouth can be an offence these days. Or perhaps the chairman does have something to hide, and finds that fluffing his meaning helps. Either way, you need to decode the message, or perhaps clarify it in a chat after the annual meeting.

The future is what matters. Look hard at anything under the heading 'Prospects' for reservations, qualifications, or modifications. They will not be there by accident. The wording will be intended to give the chairman an excuse to say 'I warned you' if something should go wrong, even if he has said something like 'Prospects appear excellent, and the company will continue to grow strongly while demand is sustained.' Er, um, excuse me. 'While demand is sustained?' What does that mean? Is it a sneaky way of saying that we do not know what is happening to orders, they may not stretch too far ahead, and we could be in trouble if they fall?

Talk of 'continuing growth' could refer to sales, trading profits, pre-tax profits, or earnings. What matters most is earnings per share. 'Expansion' is another vague word. Does it mean issuing lots of shares? Or will existing businesses do better and grow? If there was heavy capital spending last year, will it bring higher profits this year? Or is expansion of sales concealing a fall in profits?

If there is no mention of growth, will there be any? Chairmen should give some guidance in the report, or at the annual meeting. What is left unsaid could be more important than what is said. Talk of rationalisation means some part of the business is not going well. Will closing or cutting it back mean an exceptional charge? Will it be taken above the line (out of pre-tax profits and earnings per share), or below (set off against reserves, where analysts might not worry so much and the dividend will not be threatened)?

Mention of 'increased competition' almost invariably means lower margins and falling profits. Does it mean actual losses? 'Market share' can be tricky, too. Is the market itself growing? Or is the company seeing lower sales, and raising market share by clinging on in a market which is falling? 'Currency changes' may influence profits, and could mean assets have to be written down – or up. Total candour is rare indeed when it means explaining to investors that things are going wrong, and the business is falling apart. Companies almost always put the best interpretation they can on absolutely anything. So if you are worried, and the message is not clear to you, never hesitate to ask. It is your money at stake.

CREATIVE ACCOUNTING

You can be sure the chairman will want to steer clear of questions about creative accounting. Any hint of accounting matters, and he will lob them to the finance director, or the auditors. You may get precious little satisfaction or sense out of them.

In these sophisticated times, it can come as a shock to be told that company profits, duly audited by the nation's finest and most expensive accountancy brains and certified as complying with the Companies Act, may be far from what they seem. Companies have great flexibility in deciding what is, and what is not, a profit or a loss. It is all due to accounting standards, and can be quite baffling for even the most advanced investors.

Because relatively few really understand accounting, it does not have a vast impact on share prices. It often hovers somewhere between fact and fiction, a vague impression that some accounts are not to be trusted quite so much as others. A full understanding might help you avoid some of the dodgier companies, but their problems will generally be spotted elsewhere in time for you to heed the warning of a falling share price, and to sell then.

For the average investor, it may be enough to listen for talk about things like off balance sheet financing. That means the company is arranging borrowings in associated companies in a fashion which does not show up readily in the published report and accounts. The company may have mortgaged the future more heavily than you realise, and may be legally responsible for more debt than you imagined, if things go wrong. In future, this should be less of a problem. New accounting standards, set up to tackle many of the more obvious tricks, decree that such borrowings should now be in the accounts.

Then there are items which inflate profits by counting income on a long-term contract in different proportions at different stages of completing the contract. Companies can juggle with the allocation of costs, capitalising them. This means the cost of work is assumed to have added value to an asset, and can be written into the balance sheet as a plus, instead of being taken off profits as a minus. Wonderful. The most commonly capitalised item is interest – the cost of the money property companies borrow while they are building something, and which they expect to recover when the completed building is eventually sold. That works well, until the building has to be sold at a loss.

There is also the well-established game of splitting extraordinary items and exceptional items. Extraordinary items can be taken directly to reserves, instead of the profit tally. Because they are one-off, and will not happen again, they should not be allowed to distort the real trend, so the argument runs. An exceptional item is not quite extraordinary, but can be taken above the line, in the profits, though it may not necessarily happen again.

Would you believe it? It is amazing how many extraordinary items turn out to be losses, and go to reserves instead of the profit and loss account. And so many exceptional items are gains, which qualify for inclusion in the profit and loss account. Heigh-ho. This is another game being tackled by new accounting standards. Watch how it works.

Then there are provisions. These little beauties crop up frequently when a company has been active in acquiring others. The buyer makes a special provision against the cost of reorganising the newly-bought business. In subsequent years, it can gradually take these provisions back, setting them off against the costs which are actually incurred, as they arise. The scope for taking running costs out of the profit and loss account, and thus transforming them into a less sensitive balance sheet item, is wonderful. Too many losses, of course, dent the profit record and the share rating. Busy companies would not be able to persuade the City to back them to make more bids.

There are games galore a shrewd finance director can play, all with the blessing of accountants. The main worry comes when the games start attracting comment, and begin to undermine the share price. Sometimes, of course, the tricks build the equivalent of an unexploded bomb, storing up potential problems that could lead to massive losses if it all goes wrong. For most purposes, you need not worry too much. It only really counts when the City begins to worry about what is going on, and it hits the share price. When that starts, do not wait. Sell at once. It will only get worse.

TALKING TO YOUR BROKER

Talking to your stockbroker, if you have one, can be an art in itself. Never forget, he has an angle. He lives on the commission he earns buying and selling shares, so he likes you to trade. He also lives on capital gains from trading shares for himself, so there are times when it will suit him for you to buy a particular share to help push the price up. And since the Big Bang, the shares he suggests you buy might be owned by his firm – though he should tell you. So remember our earlier note about the difference between agents and principals. Agents act for you, and do not hold shares themselves. Principals act for you, but may set the prices and may own the shares you buy or sell.

If your broker comes up with a share for you to buy, ask why. There may be a written report on it from his research department, with profit projections, dividend forecasts, price earnings ratios, asset value, and so on. Such reports can be brilliant. Or they may be third-rate. Try to talk to the analysts, and note what they say. Ask where the shares are coming from, and how many there are. If they are part of a large line, perhaps someone interesting – a director or a major shareholder – is selling. Why? Usually, of course, the shares will not be coming from anywhere special, and your broker will deal in the normal way through a market-maker.

In general, it is not a good idea to trade on your broker's gossip, unless you know him extremely well. A new boy, anxious to impress, may give you his best ideas, but his inexperience may tell. A more senior broker will give his best ideas to his biggest clients first.

And remember, brokers take less risk when they deal for themselves, because they pay no commission, and are in touch minute by minute. Today's favourite may be old news for them tomorrow. They may have been in and moved on out, while you are still wondering what is happening. If you contact a broker with an idea, ask what he thinks and what his research department makes of it. Several bigger firms provide predictions across a remarkable range of companies, either in books which are regularly updated, or on computer screens. You may get a frosty response if you are a small trader, but it is worth trying. Ask him to check the price and size (the number of shares you can trade in) with all of the market-makers (prices do differ a little from place to place). A good broker will do this automatically, getting the best for you.

WHAT YOUR BROKER REALLY MEANS

Informed, independent and urbane though he may appear, your broker is merely a tradesman, there to do your bidding. You pay the bill. But he also often owes a duty to some of the companies whose shares he trades. All quoted companies have a stockbroking firm to advise them. That firm will usually produce reports on the company's progress, and be the best-informed source of profit forecasts. Most often, comment will be favourable. The verdict will rarely be 'Sell'. That could cost the broker a valuable customer, and a handy retainer.

Even if your broker is not official broker to a particular company, his research department has to tread delicately. Whatever a broker may say in private, he has to be careful about his public stance – witness the remarkable ability of Smith New Court to act for Robert Maxwell while quietly telling valued customers to sell the shares.

Stockbroking analysts can ask penetrating questions of companies, and some are impressively well-informed. Unlike financial journalists, they cannot try to insist on answers. They rely for their information on the company's goodwill. So when it comes to making less than glowing comments, brokers must be careful. If they tell clients to sell, or point to a problem, that company may refuse to speak to the analyst again. Analysts need to be able to talk to companies to get the extra, inside information which will allow them to give advice.

Make no mistake, company brokers ARE given inside information. They are used deliberately to channel good news to the big investors. Or, when the company itself cannot be seen to do it directly, they are encouraged to soften the blow of bad news by filtering the word quietly around the City.

The upshot of all of this is that brokers often speak in riddles. Written comments sometimes appear in a code, because it would be unwise to say what they really mean. On other occasions, they simple get so tangled in clever technical analysis that they are almost incapable of putting it into plain English, or assessing what it means for the share price.

So look at brokers' circulars with a jaundiced eye, and talk to them with care. Try to decipher the real message. Only slightly tongue-in-cheek, this may help.

* *Strong Buy* . . . My neck is on the line if we do not get the price up

* *Buy* . . . Should be all right

* *Buy for income* . . . Do not expect much capital gain

* *Buy for the long term* . . . Something may turn up

* *Buy/Hold* . . . We are brokers to the company. They would be upset if we did not say buy

* *Look to buy* . . . It may go down, so do not touch it now

* *Buy for recovery* . . . We hope the fall has stopped

* *Take Overweight Position* . . . Probably a buy, but we do not want anyone to criticise us if it goes down

* *Undervalued Opportunity* . . . Nothing has happened for ages. The directors say the shares are too low. They always say that

* *Strong Hold* . . . Who knows?

* *Hold* . . . Nothing happening. Sell

* *Weak hold* . . . Sell at once

* *Reduce Weighting* . . . Sell the lot

* *Look to sell* . . . may go up a little. Get out if you have any sense

* *Good technical position* . . . Our chartist thinks it looks cheap, but what does he know?

* *Weak technical position* . . . our chartist says it is dear. Who knows?

* *Our forecast is being raised* . . . the company swears business is good, and another broker has raised his forecast

* *Our forecast is being reduced* . . . we got it wrong. We have already told our best clients to sell

*   *Bid possibilities are in the price for nothing* . . . take a gamble
*   *Ambitious expansion programme* . . . watch for a flood of new shares

SETTING LIMITS

Always give your broker clear instructions on the number of shares to trade, and what you expect to pay or get. Be sure whether he is to deal 'at best' – whatever price he can get – or 'on limits' – only at a price you set. If you do set limits, make them clear, and be prepared not to trade if your broker cannot meet them. Sometimes he will be able to leave your limits with the market-maker, perhaps for days, and he will deal if the price hits them. This gives dealers a useful target, and can help you get a better price, but it does not always work. Where you are trying to buy shares with a wide spread between buying and selling price, it may be worth setting limits close to the middle price. Give your broker something to work for, if he will take such an order.

Make it clear, too, whether your broker can deal at his discretion, or only on your instructions. A good broker can save you money by trading quickly if he sees an opportunity, and uses his discretion on individual trades. But you need to trust each other, and it is no good giving your broker discretion and complaining if his judgement turns out wrong.

Do not give anyone blanket discretion to trade all of your share cash, or all of your portfolio. That way, you may find you are pumped full of the old rubbish the firm needs to shift. Do not give discretion to anyone who approaches you over the phone with investment ideas. And never deposit cash with a broker you do not know well, and leave him to deal on it. If you sell something, make sure the cash comes back to you. Do not leave it on account with the broker, no matter how safe and convenient he may suggest that would be.

NARROW MARKETS

Never buy more shares than the market-maker will normally trade at the stated price. If you do, it could be difficult to sell. You may not be able to deal at the market price, especially if prices are falling. If the price quoted is in 5,000 shares, do not buy 10,000 unless you are ready to take an extra risk, and prepared to be patient about getting out.

If the market-makers quote a price for a relatively small package, with a wide spread between buying and selling rates – say, more than 4pc – take extra care. You have found a narrow market stock.

This can be magic when the price is rising, because it responds sharply to modest buying. Whereas you can trade in £250,000 worth of ICI shares without the price blinking, there are shares which move 5pc or more on a deal worth £1,000. Many more move 5pc on deals worth £5,000. These are generally shares in small, speculative companies. But not always.

Narrow market shares are killers when the price turns down. This usually happens more rapidly and savagely than a rise. The moment they sense extra selling, market-makers hammer the price. They do not want to get caught holding stock in a little company which attracts modest trade, and which may spring a nasty surprise.

It is a brave, or foolish, investor who weighs in heavily for a narrow market stock. Seeing it go up, it can be tempting to buy more. Be warned. The real disaster for small punters and other gamblers in the Crash of 1987 was finding that they literally could not sell some companies at any price. If your broker says your favourite stock is a narrow market, think again. You need to be doubly sure when you walk on the wild side.

CHEAP AT THE PRICE

Hard to believe, but there are brokers who will peddle you the line that certain shares are cheap because they were once much dearer. I hear it from unsophisticated investors, and naive journalists, too. Perhaps weariness takes over and they stop thinking. Do not get caught. If you study the highs and lows, and see that a share is 100p below the peak, it is tempting to think that it might go back up again one day. After all, somebody once thought it worth 100p extra, and actually paid it. It must have looked right then. Perhaps it just drifted back by chance?

Forget it. Shares do fall out of favour, and prices do suffer from neglect at times. But there is usually a reason. Somebody else knows it. Circumstances have changed. If the price goes back towards the peak, there will be sellers all the way up, relieved at the chance to break even and write off a mistake.

LISTEN TO THE PRICE

Listen to what the share price is telling you. It is a valuable lesson. Before you buy, watch for a while. Get a feel for the range it trades in, how sharply it rises, the way it falls. Watch closely on days when the market is moving strongly one way or another. If it falls when all else is rising, be wary. If it rises when others fall, or holds steady, someone may be accumulating stock, confident enough to pick it up through thick and thin. Smart dealers know how to build a stake without attracting attention. They try to buy when the market is falling, lay off to let sellers come in, and pick up stock again when the price slips.

Get your broker to try to check with the market-maker. A good broker may be able to wheedle out whether the buying is consistently from one source. He may even glean some idea of price parameters. When the big boys are buying, you may be able to tag along for the ride.

Shares do tend to get a momentum going. Do not fight it. If a share keeps sliding gently, be suspicious. If you are determined to buy, wait for it to find a level. It is worth sacrificing 10pc or so to make sure the fall is over. Let someone else risk buying at the bottom. Equally, there are times when a rise goes steadily on and up. It is always hard to guess where it will stop. Stay with it while it lasts, if you can time it correctly.

DOUBLE BOTTOMS AND PLUNGING NECKLINES – THE CHARTS

There are people who live by charts, who swear they tell you the true share story. They shut their eyes to fundamentals – such things as profits and dividends – and watch dots or crosses on graph paper, and reckon the real action is there, plain to see.

It is easy to mock. One of the noisiest names in the business used his charts to recommend one company less than a fortnight before the receiver moved in. Had he spoken to the brokers, or looked at the accounts, he would have known what dire straits the company was in before he wrote. Now he checks the fundamentals before going overboard on chart tips. There is another side to the coin. Jim Slater, the share king of the sixties and early seventies, was asked at one annual meeting of Slater Walker what he thought of chartists who said his shares were too high. He answered scornfully that chartists tended to have ragged raincoats and big overdrafts. A few years later, Slater Walker crashed. Jim himself became our best-known minus millionaire for a while.

Charts can be a valuable aid, if you are first familiar with the investment basics. They do give an idea of what other investors think, and sometimes show what the insiders are doing. Once you have found a sound share, there is no harm in seeing what the charts say. Most brokers have a chartist tucked away. And you can watch for their views in the press, or in specialist services.

WHAT CHARTISTS DO

Chartists draw patterns around share price moves. Some follow the closing price each day, marking it on a vertical scale, with the time period on the horizontal. Others make bar charts, placing a little vertical line to cover the high and low trading range for the day, with a horizontal line for the closing level.

Point and figure charts are more ambitious. These focus on significant price movements, with a vertical row of crosses for each worthwhile gain, and noughts for each fall. There is no set time-scale. A new column is formed with each change of direction.

The chartist sees a pattern in the dots and lines. A double bottom shows a price falling to a low, rising, and finally falling back to that low. This might mean the shares will go no lower. It might mean someone is buying at a particular level, and this the chart watcher can follow.

On the other hand, a double bottom might become a triple bottom. Or even a false bottom, followed by a lower bottom. Turn bottoms upside down, and they become tops – points at which shares stop rising, and a seller always seems to hit the price.

Plunging necklines catch the eye of the chartist in a falling market. A neckline is a support level below a head and shoulders formation. Leave it to the experts to determine what that is, along with flags, spear points, rectangles, reverse heads and shoulders, and other exotica.

Around all of these, chartists arrive at conclusions on trends and momentum. Ask, and you may be told a trend is a trend until it stops. That sums up a great deal about chart watching. It gives a glimpse of what is going on, sort of, but it is of limited use for what you really want to know – what happens next.

THE VALUE OF CHARTS

Charts do count, however, because people pay attention to them. No matter how daft it may seem, anything is important if it prompts people to buy or sell. Talk about support points and resistance levels means chartists think it will be important if a share – or perhaps the market – moves beyond a particular level. They may be telling clients that if the Financial Times Index falls below 1,800, an important support has been breached, and a slump could follow. Some clients may take notice and sell, so the prediction becomes self-fulfilling. You may not heed it, but it is as well to be aware of what is going on.

Charts are handy, too, to show what people have been paying for shares. And to give an idea of the likely mass of buyers or sellers. If a lot bought shares at around a particular level, it matters. Usually, the charts show where it happened, with the price hovering around that level for quite a while. When a price is falling, previous experience may indicate a support point, the level at which investors are more prone to buy.

Where a share is rising, signs that it once hovered around a particular price may indicate a potential resistance level, where many bought earlier, saw a fall, and may get out when they see their money back. It may be significant if the price goes above this resistance. Potential sellers may be exhausted, and future buyers could find the shares in shorter supply, so they will rise more rapidly. In a falling market, the reverse may happen. If a share drops through a support level, where there have been ready buyers in the past, potential new buyers may be put off, and sellers will hit the price harder.

Such an outline does scant justice to what has become a very sophisticated affair, but it will suffice for many investors. Chartists would be more convincing if they could muster greater agreement among themselves over the meaning of charts. Ask half a dozen about the same chart, and you could get six different views. That, as they say, is what makes a market. If you want to learn more, the classic chartist text book is *Technical Analysis of Stock Trends*, by Edwards & McGee.

NO-ONE LEFT TO BUY

Charts can help clarify some of the rules the professionals keep in mind, especially relating to the particular characteristics some shares develop. It all goes back to instinct, developing a feel.

Watch, and you will see how some shares never make much progress, no matter how impressive the fundamentals.

Year in, year out, analysts used to estimate that the asset value of the multinational Lonrho was four or five times greater than the share price, that profits were rising, and that the dividend yield was into double figures, way above average. Nevertheless, the shares stuck in a narrow trading range.

You either loved or hated Lonrho chief executive Tiny Rowland. In 1985, Lonrho began to power ahead, breaking out of the price trap, pushing up in 1986. After years of stagnation, they had found a new generation of buyers, young fund managers ready to buy a high-yielder with prejudice from long-established City doubts about the company. Until then, every believer had the shares. The rest did not want to know at any price. There was no-one left to buy, no matter how bright the business looked.

Shares do run out of buyers. They learn to live with their rating. The market grows used to seeing some shares on a low PE, and others on a high one. They get left alone, indiscriminately. It can take a major change to shift traders' perceptions. Only the big boys will bring it about. Watch for it starting, and try to ride with it then. Stay away until you are sure the change is coming.

LATE NEWS

Be wary of announcements which come late. Bad figures almost invariably take longer to add up than good ones. Companies often announce the date of profit statements in advance, but there is no firm rule. Usually, they roll around at about the same point each year, so keep an eye on your diary. Any statement more than three weeks overdue should be viewed with suspicion. Ask your broker if he knows the reason. Or try ringing the company secretary. It might be safest not to wait. If in doubt, sell out.

ONE PRODUCT COMPANIES

Take special care with one product companies, or companies which depend for a large slice of their business on one customer. There are not too many about these days. But when the competition comes along, as it surely will , they can crumble fast.

And be imaginative. Ratners the jewellers may not strike you immediately as the retail equivalent of a one product company. But in the UK and the USA, it got stuck with a down-market cut-price image, even though it had a number of better-class stores. When the fun started to fade for cheaper jewellery, the impact was devastating. Suddenly chairman Gerald Ratner found himself hoist on his own petard, condemned all round as the cut-price king, with nowhere to go but down.

CHAPTER TWELVE
THE CRUCIAL MOVE – SELLING SHARES

It is easy to buy a share, much harder to sell it. Somehow parting with an investment is a more emotional affair than picking it in the first place. Investors can be remarkably patient with a tipster who gets it wrong, picks a share which falls. But tell someone to take profits on a favourite which promptly goes higher, and the complaints come loud and long. I know it. Hell hath no fury like a winner scorned.

Selling, though, is the essential second half of any successful investment deal. It is no good spotting winner after winner if you are hanging on when the market turns, and everything tumbles out of bed, the good with the bad. The only profits which count are the ones you take, the ones you bank by selling winners while you are ahead. Paper profits are for the birds.

There is one classic, all-time investment rule. CUT YOUR LOSSES QUICKLY, AND LET YOUR PROFITS RUN. Everybody knows it. Almost everyone ignores it. There is a natural tendency to sell winners to finance losers – to do just the opposite of what you should. Investors are surprisingly devoted to duds, reluctant to accept that they have got it wrong, and that the best way out is the quickest.

CUTTING YOUR LOSSES

Do it. CUT YOUR LOSSES. Experts count themselves content if they pick six winners out of ten – anything better is a bonus. It may sound wimpish, until you try to do it. It may even be a trifle conservative in a bull market, when everything is rising. But it is not unrealistic. Pick more winners than losers, and you must come out ahead unless you are stupid. You will certainly come out ahead if you make it an unbudging rule to sell losers while the losses are small, and to hold winners while the profits are piling up.

It is obvious, so elementary that it hardly needs saying. Sadly, years of talking to investors, reading their letters, listening to their excuses, make it plain that few people heed it. CUT, CUT, CUT YOUR LOSSES QUICKLY.

Everyone will have their own idea of what cutting losses quickly means. Time does not matter. Linger as long as you like, but move swiftly once the loss starts to mount up. It sounds like a cop-out, but YOU MUST SET A SELLING TARGET. Promise yourself to sell if your shares fall beyond a certain level, and set this selling point when you buy. Set it sensibly. Make it between 10pc and 20pc below your buying price, less if you are an aggressive investor.

At this point, it is tempting to start screaming. I have just given you the best investment advice you will ever have. It is worth a fortune – if you follow it. It is the most important thing in this whole book. Yet most investors ignore it. Please do not join them.

No-one buys a share with the idea of losing money. The sensible investor admits the possibility. Keep a stop-loss figure in your head. Ask your broker about it. Some brokers will take stop-loss levels, and try to work with them. Others may rely on you to tell them when you should sell. Do it.

THE STOP-LOSS SYSTEM

Prudent investors will go further than simply placing a stop-loss order to prevent large losses. Although it takes some of the romance out of investment, eliminating the thrill of imagining you are driving brilliantly by the seat of your pants, you should operate a fully-fledged stop-loss system – to cover winners and losers.

Never mind that it is called a stop-loss system. It might as well be called a save-profits system. Or anything you like. Just follow it.

It may sound a trifle complicated, but once you get used to the idea, it is simplicity itself. It also has the virtue of encouraging you to watch prices each day, so you develop a better feel for what is happening.

When you buy a share, set a price at which you will sell should it fall, following the simple stop-loss rule outlined above. As the price rises, move your potential selling point up behind it – a trailing stop-loss. Never cheat. NEVER, NEVER LOWER YOUR STOP-LOSS PRICE.

Say you buy at 100p. Set your first stop-loss price at 80p. If it falls that far, sell, and write that share off.If the price rises to 110p, raise your stop-loss level to 90p. If it goes to 120p, trail the stop-loss price up behind it to 100p. And so on.

If the shares go to 150p, your stop-loss price should be 130p. Then if there is a market slump, or something goes wrong with that particular share, you will have sold at 130p to clinch a

30pc profit. You may have missed the top, but you will not be left worried and miserable, with no profit at all, if the price slides back to 100p – or 90p, or less.

The disadvantage of the system is clear. You never get out at the top. And selling at the top really can give you a warm, superior glow. Remember, though, the old market legend about the Rothschild who made his fortune by selling too soon – but always at a profit.

The system is not infallible – no system is. There are times when it will take you out of super stocks too soon. It may leave you nursing a loss on a potential winner which takes off the instant you sell it. Just such a thing happened in the mid-eighties when I wrote a regular tipping column in the Daily Mail on each Saturday. Every tip was accompanied by a stop-loss price. I fancied Alan Sugar's Amstrad just as he introduced his big-selling word processor, and tipped the shares. Within weeks, I was forced to apologise, and suggest readers should follow my advice and take a stop-loss of just under 20pc, selling in the 70p range. Almost immediately after, Amstrad took off like a rocket. I had spotted one of the year's big success stories, but got my timing competely wrong, and managed to advise some three million Daily Mail readers on how to lose money on it. Great.

That never shook my faith in the system. I gave up the tipping column in 1986, worried about the frothy nature of the market. It did not seem right tipping shares when things could so easily go wrong. Once again, my timing was off. The Great Crash did not happen until October 1987, though the market peaked some months earlier. When the Crash came, I could rest secure that no Daily Mail reader should have been left with massive losses on my tips. Every one should have used their stop-loss system to cut losses quickly, or should have trailed the selling level up as the shares went higher. Most should have been able to get out at a useful profit.

Clever? Not really. Elementary. But, above all, a responsible approach to playing the market. Sadly, I overlooked it later with Polly Peck. I had picked Polly as my share of the year for 1990, and suggested a stop loss price. Anyone who followed that would have got out with a good profit before Polly tumbled in the autumn. Fine.

Foolishly, I tipped Polly again in June 1990, near the peak, without suggesting a stop-loss. As the crisis hit, I found it hard to believe the shares would not bounce back. Instead of advising readers to cut their losses, I suggested holding on. The shares were suspended, and now look worthless. It was a stupid mistake. I had forgotten my own rule, become blinded by past success tipping the stock, and too much influenced by my regard for chairman Asil Nadir.

It is easy to make mistakes, and easy to see them now. I tell the story to hammer home the stop-loss message. It is tempting to plead that certain stocks are special, favourites, ones you know especially well. Forget it. Stick to the system, no matter what. It is much the safest way to play.

It would be possible to quote one example after another, back to the early seventies when I started using the system,. Bob Beckman, the source of so many valuable investment pointers, taught me about it. In truth, I ignored it in my personal investments until the late eighties. Then I began to follow it. Though there was one period when I regretted selling stock just before a rally, a few months later I was blessing it. With hindsight it saved me a great deal of money.

Do it, and it will ensure that you come out ahead, provided you pick more winners than losers. It must. This simple system means your losses are relatively small, and your gains are bigger.

You will still lose money when you get things wrong. The system ignores dealing costs, which take a bite out of all of your investments. And there may be times when you cannot sell at your stop-loss level, because the price falls too quickly. Do not be deflected. Sell at the highest price you can, once your stop-loss has been breached.

You can introduce a degree of refinement if the market is edgy, or if you are playing a particularly volatile stock. Clearly, slower-moving shares do not always require a full 20pc discount when you set the stop-loss. It might be better to set a stop-loss 10pc, or 15pc below the buying price.

You can refine the system as your profits grow. Obviously a 20pc discount of 20p on a 100p price is equivalent to a 10pc discount by the time the price rises to 200p. You might be happy to accept that finer margin. Or you might want to re-set the stop-loss at 160p. Cutting the stop-loss in that way is not unreasonable when you are on a big winner and are tempted to stay with it. But never abandon the stop-loss altogether.

On the other hand, you might grow more nervous as the price goes higher. You might want a tighter stop-loss. If the market is overheating, it might be sensible to close all of your stop-loss settings tighter behind the price, bidding goodbye at the first real setback. Use your own judgement.

SELLING HALF

There are other selling systems. Most popular is the notion of selling half when a share doubles. Pick a big winner, and you can end up with one stock dominating your portfolio. It is a nice problem to have.

The traditional approach imagines that is is a problem, and that you really ought to sell half so that your original holding has cost you nothing, and you have a free ride, reinvesting your profit in something else. Nonsense. That is no way to make a killing. Finding a real winner is not easy. When you do, stick with it. The market always tends to overdo things, and your rocket may soar to a silly height before it begins to fade. You could see the price multiply three or four-fold, maybe much more. Never sell a share while it is still flying.

Ths stop-loss system is the ideal way of making the most of such a star. Do not get off until it starts to fall. By all means cheat. Once a share has doubled, allow more lee-way and trail the stop-loss behind at a bigger discount, if you fancy. Bigger profits allow a more relaxed approach.

But do sell when it begins to fail. Never fall blindly in love with a share. Try asking yourself if you would buy it if you had just stumbled across it for the first time. That can be a very sobering exercise. Suddenly you realise you may be sitting with a share with a PE of 30 or more, not something you would touch normally – and certainly the kind of rating which will cause potential new buyers, the ones who will push the price still higher, to worry about whether it is too high to buy.

SELL SIGNALS

Unless you have a system, deciding when to sell is a real problem. No bell rings when a share hits the top. Try turning upside down the rules you used when you decided to buy. Ask yourself if what attracted you then still holds good. If the PE has grown too far out of line with the average for the sector, or the yield has shrunk, you may wonder whether you should hold on. When you sell, you will need to find a buyer, someone who thinks the shares are a bargain. If the averages are too far out of line, that might be difficult.

Watch the price momentum, too. You do not need a system to understand that, once a share hits a peak and begins to stutter, it has lost momentum. You have to judge how long that will last, and whether it will regain it. Logically it may not make much sense, but potential buyers are attracted to a rising share. They see the strong price as a demonstration of confidence – if others are buying, they must know something. And when a price starts to fall, there is always a nasty feeling that someone knows something bad that you cannot see. That may be right.

THE PRIVATE INVESTOR'S ADVANTAGES

The private investor has a few important advantages over the big boys, especially when it comes to selling. You are responsible to no-one but yourself. There is no committee to report to, no trustees checking what you do, no shareholders, fundholders, policyholders. You get it wrong, or you get it right. No-one is going to censure you, demote you, fire you. You do not have to be in the fashionable stocks of the day, nor must you avoid certain sectors which are out of favour. The impact of press comment need not matter. No-one is going to say you cannot do just what you want.

That can be worth a lot. It is part of the invaluable flexibility you have as a small investor. YOU DO NOT HAVE TO BE IN THE MARKET WHEN THINGS LOOK BAD. Big investors have to have much of their money there all of the time. They have to take the long view. There is considered to be nowhere else big enough to take their cash. They are always ready to recommend patience to others. They do not want everyone else to sell while they are stuck in. If they all withdrew – or tried to – the stock market would be finished. Prices would crash, and their own performance would be hammered. They would slitting their own throats, lining themselves up for redundancy. Everyone has an angle, remember? Their angle is that they need to get prices up and keep them up, to keep their jobs. Their power to manipulate the market to that end may be limited by economic circumstance, and they cannot be absolute dictators. But they can go a long way towards it.

You have no such worries. And you can buy and sell much more easily. Large investors have trouble buying all of the shares they seek sometimes, and have to be wary of pushing prices up against themselves. Crucially, they can have real trouble selling. They have such a large position in so many shares that they would wallop the price out of sight if they tried to unload. When they have 3pc or more of a company, every move has to be reported. Imagine the impact of a major investor cutting from 4.5pc to 3pc of a market leader when the going turned tougher. That would smash the price. The big boys cannot always do what they know they should. You can.

They also get caught by the inside information which often helps them. Once they know something is going on, they are supposed not to sell. Though there are obvious fuzzy areas around the edges, that can be a burden. They may know bad news is coming, but they have to sit tight. And must plod on, backing any reconstruction, when they know it might take years for the price to recover.

There are no such inhibitions for the private investor. The news may come a little later, and the price may have started to fall, but the individual can kiss a dud goodbye quickly, leaving it to struggle. The small player is rarely locked in. FLEXIBILITY IS WORTH A FORTUNE. Make the most of it.

IF IN DOUBT, SELL OUT

Conventional clap-trap about whether the market takes too much of a short-term view need not trouble you. Always err on the side of safety. IF IN DOUBT, SELL OUT.

The notion that the long term investor does better than the quick in and out merchant has always seemed highly dubious. If making profits is your prime concern, there is no merit in holding for ten years while the market goes through an up cycle, back down, and then up again – just before it turns down. The cycles do exist. Take advantage of them, even if you only switch into cash and earn boring fixed interest in the dull phase. Better that than to see capital values crashing. Cash will buy you so much more at the bottom than at the top. The long term holder only does better than the in and out merchant (who does incur more dealing costs) if the stayer picks a good stock, and the sprinter does one dud deal after another. Common sense says so.

If you do take a long term view, then, be trebly certain that you have picked a winner. And be ready to face hefty losses as you go. The best stocks move with the market. At some stage, almost all will be well below their peak.

Only you can decide what suits you. Always err on the side of safety. October 1987 made nonsense of a lot of long term resolutions. Gains which had taken years to accumulate were wiped out in a couple of days. Stocks did rally, and the market was hiting new peaks four years later. But many leaders had still not recovered, and hundreds of medium to small stocks were still in a sorry state. Every day you are in the market, you are taking a risk. THE LONGER YOU HOLD, THE GREATER THE RISK. Who knows what is just over the horizon?

Do not be content to sit with a share which is quietly slipping away. Put a price limit, or a time limit on your patience. Decide how far you will let it fall before you sell, or how long you will wait for a rise. If the price is becalmed, then begins to ease, sell. Ask yourself if you would not be doing better in something else. Take your cash and keep it safe while you worry.

If you are awake, the main selling signal usually comes from the price itself. Watch if it fails to go up, or slips when others are rising. Unless you know why it is not responding, sell.

A MARKET SLUMP

If you think the whole market is headed for a fall, sell it all, no matter how bright the prospects may be for your favourite. Few shares buck a falling market. It is easy to get caught up watching individual prices, and to miss the signs of a general slump. Watch the indices, the Financial Times Stock Exchange 100 Share Index. Watch predictions in the press, talk of economic gloom, a sterling crisis, a change of government. Take your money and run to a building society or the National Savings Investment Account until the storm blows over.

WATCHING THE COMPETITION

There may be individual sell signs from the competition. If one brewer gives notice of a bad summer, others will be suffering. If terrorist bombs keep them away from the Savoy, then Forte will be feeling the pain, too. Look for allied industries. When house sales slump, it is not just housebuilders who get hurt. Estate agents, brickmakers, kitchen companies, carpet makers, do-it-yourself firms and so on feel the pinch. So do the banks, building societies, and second mortgage companies.

BOARD-ROOM BUST-UPS

A board-room bust-up can be a sell sign. There may be bad profits to come, and someone is carrying the can. Generally, though, it is good news. The problems will normally have been spotted already in the stock market, and there will be relief that something is being done about them. Or the split could make the company more vulnerable to a bid, especially if the board change involves someone with a significant share stake.

SELL AHEAD OF AN ANNOUNCEMENT

Always be prepared to sell ahead of a company announcement, rather than after it. The market almost always overdoes things. Anticipation is the most rewarding part of most investment – unless you spot a bid. Each Saturday or Monday, most City pages list the main board meetings in the week ahead. Prices frequently rise in the weeks before the meetings, if all is going well. Check, and if you are trading for the short term, or thinking of selling, do it ahead of the announcement.

By the time you see it in the newspapers, any news will be known all over the City, and the shares will have reacted. You will often find that others bought in anticipation. and sold once the news appeared. That is why many shares fall on what seems to be good news. It would have taken something extra special to bring a further gain.

SELLING ON A TIP

Every now and then, shares take a great leap forward for no apparent reason. They may have been tipped in a newsletter, in the press, or by some stockbroker. If a good broker is getting behind them, stay aboard. If it is a tipsheet, or some press pundit, read what they have to say, and make up your own mind. It may be a good selling opportunity, taking advantage of a temporary surge while the tipster's fans climb aboard. For that reason, think twice before selling on a Friday. The weekend press usually carries a shower of tips, and your share could open with a nice Monday morning boost.

Friday is rarely a good day to sell. Every two weeks, it will mark the end of a Stock Exchange trading account. Some account speculators will have had to scramble out to avoid taking stock up and paying for it. Market-makers see them coming, and mark prices down accordingly. There may be a recovery after 3.30, however, when late dealings qualify for the new account.

SELL IN MAY

The market is full of old sayings. Most make some sense. 'Sell in May and go away' is a favourite. It has worked more often than not in recent years. Because the tax year ends early in April, some investors wait to take profits in the new tax year, shunting tax payments a year further forward, or using up the gains-free exemption for the new year.

As May winds on, the City sneaks into summer. People go on holiday, Parliament is quiet, there is Wimbledon, Ascot, Henley, and a host of free tickets and parties to tempt fund managers from their desks. Most companies end their financial year on December 31, or March 31. The December year-end brigade report profits around March and April. March year-end profits tend to come out by the middle of June. So mid-summer is quieter for company news. If you do sell in May, think about buying towards the second half of August. Business begins to return to normal in September.

BETTING AGAINST THE CROWD

Contrary thinking, or betting against the crowd, is another favourite. It usually gains most prominence as a sign to sell.

Often it is used as a sneer to mock the small investor, with the suggestion that when the small players arrive in force, it is time for professionals to sell. It has become such a cliche that the whole idea is losing appeal. But it can work if applied carefully. The bigger the crowd, the fewer there are left to join in. Share prices need a constant flow of new buyers to push them up.

Be careful, though. The crowd creates the winners. So contrary thinking requires caution. Use it to make sure that you look hard before leaping on any bandwagon. Check where it started rolling. The further it has come, the nearer the end it will be. Try not to be last aboard. Sensible contrary thinking means you consider both sides before making a move.

SELLING SHORT

It is easy to deal with selling short – DO NOT DO IT. Do not even think about it until you have a fat investment fortune to fall back on, and are far too sophisticated to need help from anything this book can bring you.

Professionals can make money selling short, especially in a falling market. The short seller finds a share he thinks is too high, sells, and hopes to buy it back at a lower price. He is selling shares he does not own. Sooner or later, he will have to buy an equivalent number to complete the trade. If they rise, he still has to buy them, and loses money doing it. In buying, he pushes the price up against himself, especially if he is not able to buy his full complement in one trade.

See how it works. The seller knocks out, say, 1,000 Grand Metropolitan at 540p. He does not own those shares. If they fall to, say, 500p, he can buy 1,000 to complete the deal. He has made profits of 40p a share, or £400, before expenses. However, if he has sold at 540p, and Grand Metropolitan rise, he may have to buy at 580p. He loses 40p a share, or £400, plus expenses.

When you buy a share, you can only lose as much as you have spent. Losing the lot, of course, is pretty grim. But sell short, and you cannot tell how much you might lose. Say you sell short of a share at 100p, and it suddenly gets a bid. It could rocket to 200p. You have to buy, at any price. If the market should become tight, you might have to buy at 300p, 400p, or more. That is an extreme example. But it does happen. I have watched at least two situations where the price has more than doubled as a result of a killer bear squeeze.

In the early nineties, there has been considerable publicity for a group who are said to sell shares, and then spread rumours, seeking to push the price down so that they can buy back at a profit. The name 'Evel Knievel' has been pinned to one operator. By chance, I may know him. Believe me, the man I know operates very carefully. He confines his attentions to companies where there is an inherent problem, a weak spot which could bring the price tumbling down at any time. He hit the headlines when misguided Maxwell fans in the financial press picked up and supported Robert Maxwell's bleatings about the way his shares were being sold. Do not bet against the bears. If they hit a stock you hold, the odds are that they are right. It may well be time for you to sell.

COVERED BEARS

You can go part of the way towards selling short by becoming a 'covered bear'. The covered bear picks a company where he already holds shares, and sells an equivalent number to his holding, hoping to buy them back at a lower price. If they do not fall, he is covered because he can deliver the shares he owns, completing the trade. It only makes sense if you expect shares you are holding to take a temporary dip, and then recover. Otherwise you should sell the lot, and forget them.

AVERAGING

Now and then, averaging intrudes on the scene. It is popular among unit trust managers, who see it as a handy selling tool when markets are flat. What fun, the story runs, to spend a set amount each month. When prices are low, it will buy more units, or more shares. When prices rise, you will feel the benefit, because you will have cheap units alongside the more expensive ones. It has a certain logic if you want a regular savings plan. Use it to accumulate unit or investment trusts.

Others suggest that it is a good means of making the best of a long term share stake. But it is not for the serious trader. It is simply another means of postponing a decision to take a loss. On the surface, it looks good. Buy 500 shares at 100p each, and another 500 when they have fallen to 50p, then the price only has to rise to 75p – your average – for you to be breaking even on your 1,000 shares.

Forget it. You should have sold your 100p loser at 80p. If it has halved, something is clearly wrong. It could take an age before the price recovers. You may be tossing good money after bad.

PYRAMIDING

Pyramiding resembles averaging in reverse. Averaging tends to crop up when prices are falling, pyramiding deals with rising prices. The idea is that if you buy, say 500 shares at 100p and they rise to 125p, you should ride your winner. Buy more. When your first 500 shares hit 125p, you have a paper profit of £125. If you buy another 200 shares at 125p, you will have invested a total of £750, and will hold 700 shares costing an average of just over 107p each. You will still have a profit on the lot, thanks to the safety margin from your first successful purchase. You will have more shares to profit from if they carry on up. If they fall, you can sell quickly before there is a loss.

It is an aggressive strategy which may appeal to some. Only try it if you are prepared to watch prices like a hawk. They can turn quickly. You could get caught with more shares than you had intended, and a price tumbling too fast to sell while you are ahead. Pyramiding, though, has more to commend it than averaging. At least you are trying to make the most of a winner, instead of nursing a loser.

CHAPTER THIRTEEN
GILTS, LOANS AND OTHER GAMES

Not everything on the Stock Exchange revolves around shares. More than three-quarters of stock market turnover by value is in Government Securities, or gilts as they are generally called. Up to £1bn can change hands in a single day. When interest rates are moving sharply, they can generate useful capital gains or losses, though they are widely presented as the safer end of Stock Exchange trading. Through 1991, scarcely a single gilt traded outside a range of ten points, high to low. It is not always so serene. In the first four months of 1986, when interest rates were falling sharply, some gilts scored gains of 20 points or more – heady stuff.

GILT-EDGED SECURITIES

Government securities are known as gilt-edged securities – gilts, for short – because they are backed by the government, the most reliable borrower of all, the one who (supposedly) can never go bust. Gilts are the prime source of funding for the Public Sector Borrowing Requirement (PSBR), the cash the state borrows to fund the economy. Insurance companies, pension funds and such are the biggest buyers, using them to lock in a guaranteed return to meet liabilities.

The price of gilts is always so much per £100 of stock, and £100 is the nominal value. That nominal value has a real meaning for most gilts. Unlike shares, gilts are repaid at nominal value at or between specific dates. You get £100 from the government for every £100 nominal you hold – except in the case of undated gilts, which may never be repaid. So if, early in 1991, you bought Treasury 8pc 2009 at 87, you would be repaid at £100 for each £87 worth in the year 2009.

FLAT YIELDS

The price of gilts is determined largely by interest rates. When rates fall, gilt prices rise. When rates rise, gilts fall. Buy a gilt with a 10pc coupon (the nominal interest rate it pays), standing at 100, it gives a flat yield of 10pc. If interest rates fall, the gilt price may rise to 110, where it would yield 9.09pc (10 divided by 110, multiplied by 100). If interest rates rise to 12pc, the gilt price would fall to 83, where it would yield 12pc (10 divided by 83, multiplied by 100).

REDEMPTION YIELDS

Values are complicated by the life of the gilt. Those with up to five years before they are repaid are called 'shorts'. Those with five to fifteen years of life left are 'mediums', and those with more than fifteen years left are 'longs'. A small number of stocks with no specific redemption date are 'undated'. They include the notorious War Loan, which may never be repaid.

Take, for example, 12.5pc Treasury Stock 2003 – 2005. This has a coupon of 12.5pc, and will be repaid at £100 between 2003 and 2005 (assume repayment will be at the last possible date). Because gilts sell above or below their nominal value, the repayment date is important, and influences value. The time factor is taken into account. Linked to the flat yield, it gives the redemption yield, the most widely used reference point.

Clearly if a stock is standing at 105, and will be repaid at 100 in a year's time, the holder will lose £5 capital. He will require extra income to make up for that. Conversely, if a stock is at 95, and will be redeemed at 100 in a year's time, the holder will get a capital gain of £5, and can expect less interest because of it. Gains or losses on repayment are effectively incorporated into interest payments to arrive at the redemption yield.

TAX BENEFITS

No capital gains tax is payable on gilts. So the attractions of gilts are generally related to the tax position of the purchaser. Redemption yields are generally quoted gross – before deducting tax. Only non-taxpayers get the full amount. So non-taxpayers will pick stocks with high flat yields. High taxpayers will plump for low coupon stocks with a much greater element of built-in capital gain to redemption.

INDEX-LINKED GILTS

There is another gilt complication. Since 1985, the government has been issuing index-linked gilts. Their capital repayment value rises automatically in line with inflation, as measured by the retail price index. The coupon, or nominal interest rate, is a 'real' return. It may look low at 2pc or 3pc, but you actually get that 2pc or 3pc without having to worry about the inroads inflation makes on your capital.

Because of this, an index-linked gilt may sometimes be more attractive than a conventional gilt with a similar coupon. There are index-linked gilts to cover most people's preferred time-span – short, medium, or long – and some ought to be attractive to high taxpayers. However, falling inflation rates have left index-linked gilts behind conventional ones in the quest for capital gains in many years. Somehow, they have never quite caught the imagination as they might have done.

BUYING GILTS

Trading in gilts can be complex. If you want to do it – and there are times when it may offer a haven from a stormy share market – consult a broker who understand such matters. Most firms have experts on tap. If you want to do it yourself, go to the Post Office. Many gilts can be traded over the counter with extremely low dealing costs. Gilts bought through the Post Office Register have another important advantage. The dividends are paid without tax being taken off. This saves complications for low rate taxpayers, who otherwise have to go through the tedious business of reclaiming tax. And it gives you the use of the taxable portion of the dividend for longer. It does not mean gilt dividends are free of income tax. You have to declare the interest, and pay tax on it.

GAINS FROM GILTS

Buy gilts at the right time, and they allow you to lock in a high fixed return with safety, sometimes for a very long period. If you buy when interest rates are high, and sell when they are lower, you can also secure sizeable capital gains, free of gains tax. Generally, the longer the time to redemption, the more volatile the capital value. Except with index-linked gilts, though, you face the threat of inflation, and if you get your timing wrong, could be hit by capital losses.

Buoyant share markets usually take place against a background of steady or rising gilt prices. When gilts make money, shares are offering opportunities too. Pick the right share, and you will leave the best gilt standing. Unless you think low interest rates and falling inflation are here to stay, do not buy gilts when interest rates are under 9pc. You are then likely to be near the bottom of the interest rate cycle, and could face capital losses when rates rise.

CONVERTIBLE LOAN STOCKS

There is a half-way house between the sober-sided fixed interest market and the thrills and spills of Ordinary shares – the convertible loan stock.

Convertible loan stocks carry a fixed rate of interest, a date when they will be repaid at £100 for every £100 nominal, and the opportunity to convert into Ordinary shares at certain dates. The number of shares you can switch into is fixed, and when convertibles are first issued, the terms normally let you into the Ordinary shares at a premium to the market price.

Say the Ordinary stand at 40p when the convertible is issued. That convertible may allow you to switch in three years' time into 200 Ordinary shares for every £100 of convertible loan stock – equivalent to buying 200 Ordinary at 50p each in three years' time. You will not be able to switch right away. After three years, the hope is that the Ordinary will have risen to 50p or more.

The best convertibles have a long conversion run – the chance of switching into shares over several years – but the first conversion date should not be too distant. You may be able to find convertibles which let you into the Ordinary below the current price, and give you a higher dividend return than the Ordinary in the meantime. Sometimes, of course, such apparent bargains signal something is wrong. But convertibles do occasionally get overlooked when there is a run in the shares, and sometimes a poor market in the convertible lets the price drift out of line. Pick a good one, and you get capital gains and a high return.

The theory is that the superior income on convertibles is a shelter from uncertainties in the shares. Be careful. This works sometimes, but a weak share price makes for a poor convertible price. A few points of extra interest is no consolation if your capital value tumbles as the company hits trouble. Normally you should never buy a convertible unless you are sure the shares themselves are worth buying.

The recession, though, has thrown up interesting possibilities for real punters. There are several companies whose shares have slumped, and the convertible has fallen so far that it yields well into double figures. Some of the companies are in trouble, reliant on bankers to get through the next year or two. In these cases. there is no point in buying the shares. They will have no chance of capital repayment if the company fails. The convertible might. You should switch out of the Ordinary into the convertible, if you think the company has a chance. Any capital gain will come to the convertible first, not the Ordinary.

This is another area where expert advice is worthwhile. Make sure you understand the conversion rights properly before buying. Some stocks are only partly convertible. Be sure not to let the convertible run past the conversion date without switching. That would leave you with a boring fixed interest stock, and that is no joke unless capital repayment is near, assured, and highly rewarding.

PREFERENCE PROFITS

Preference stocks are often forgotten. On the face of it, they have little to offer. They bear a fixed rate of interest, and rank ahead of Ordinary shares in their claim on dividends and assets.

The fun starts when a company hits hard times, and suspends preference dividends. Most preference capital is cumulative, which means holders are entitled to receive all of the back dividends they missed before a company can resume dividends to Ordinary shareholders. It takes a little nerve, but if you can spot cumulative preference stocks in a company with generous asset backing and the chance of a trading recovery, you could do very nicely. You could get a big slug of accumulated back dividends. Or you might find that the directors need to eliminate the preference capital in a reconstruction, and will repay it on generous terms.

Most preference stocks trade at well below their nominal value, so any capital reconstruction is likely to mean a fat profit. Preference stocks also tend to be overlooked in bid battles. They get taken over in a footnote to the main event, often at a handsome price. You might be able to buy a preference stock at £40, and see it repaid at £100.

Preference stocks are not for everyone. They can take years to come good, and can be difficult to buy and sell. But do not write them off completely.

WARRANTS

Warrants are fancy, flash relatives to convertibles. They lack the income, but can open the way to a super, low-cost, long-term gamble.

They are usually created as part of some more ambitious financing package. They act as long-life options, carrying the right to subscribe for new shares at a set price in the future. In theory, their value is calculated by reference to the price at which they allow you to buy new shares, and the date on which those shares can be bought. In practice, it is determined partly by supply and demand. Several warrants sell at prices above or below what the backroom boys impute their worth to be, using mathematical models.

HOW WARRANTS CAN BE BIG WINNERS

If you pay 20p for a warrant to subscribe for one new share at 100p, you are effectively paying 120p for that share. Generally, you will be getting in at a premium over the current price, which may only be, say, 105p. But the warrants will not let you in until some future date, when the price may be above 120p. Whatever happens, the warrant subscription price will not change, so you only pay 100p for the new share. If the market price is 200p by then, the warrant will be worth 100p (200p minus the subscription price).

That means the warrants will have gone up five-fold from your 20p purchase price, while the shares have not quite doubled from 105p. The gearing is terrific. You will have done much better in the warrants than the shares, although you miss out on the dividends.

A well-selected warrant can be a wonderful winner. Some run for 10 years or more, giving a low-priced way of buying into a growth company without tying up a lot of capital for a long time. Alternatively, they can allow you to have a much bigger interest for the same outlay – you can buy five warrants at 20p for every one share at 105p.

Once again, this is a market for the specialist. Big brokers have departments watching warrants. They are especially popular among investment trusts, where they offer a long-distance punt on the general direction of markets. Do not be put off by initial complications. You can select one, and back it yourself, no matter what the experts might say.

The danger is that warrant issues tend to be small, and the market in them can be tight. This difficulty in dealing freely in large amounts puts some big investors off. It means that when prices are rising, warrants can rise sharply – but when they fall, it can be difficult, even almost impossible, to sell. Prices fall dramatically, and losses are heavy.

ZERO COUPON SHARES AND BONDS

Relative newcomers to the UK, zero coupon bonds and preference stocks can be handy when you want to lock in a high return over a predictable period, but do not need current income. They are well suited to high rate taxpayers looking ahead to retirement. Zeros offer no fixed rate of interest, no dividend. They sell at a substantial discount to the eventual redemption price, and the interest is effectively contained in the capital appreciation which accrues as redemption approaches. Take, for example, the Gartmore Value zero. The zero started at 50p, with interest compounding monthly initially at 14pc. Projected redemption value on January 31, 1995 will be 101.1p.

There are more than twenty zero preference shares issued by investment trusts, and their ultimate value is influenced partly by how secure the performance of the trust may be. Effectively they translate income, which would be taxable, into capital gains which may escape tax if the gains are below annual exemption levels. Because they rank ahead of Ordinary shares when a trust is wound up, they ought to be relatively secure. You need to check how well the notional interest rate is covered by revenue.

TRADITIONAL OPTIONS

The glamorous and dangerous traded option market has grabbed the headlines in recent years, but traditional options still plod along, and can be a useful weapon for the gambler – a way to play in relatively large numbers of shares without laying down a fortune. Options carry the right to buy or sell a share at a set price – the 'strike' price – at some future date. Most conventional Stock Exchange options run for three months, or seven Stock Exchange trading accounts. They carry the right to buy (call options), to sell (put options), or to buy or sell (double options). The options themselves cannot be bought or sold.

It is possible to negotiate an option in most shares, at a cost of between 8pc and 15pc of the market price for calls and puts, roughly double that for doubles. When you buy, you pay stockbroking commission on the full value of the shares under option, even if you later abandon the option. When you exercise the option – use it – you pay no extra commission.

The cost of an option can only be set off against capital gains tax if it is exercised. So sometimes it is as well to exercise an option even it involves a small trading loss.

Options can be costly, but they do give you control of a lot of stock – far more than you could otherwise afford – and let you walk away if you get it wrong, losing only the cost of your option. Get it wrong, and you cannot lose more than your option money and the commission, whatever happens.

HOW A CALL OPTION WORKS

If you believe that, say, GEC will soar in the next three months, you can buy a call option on 1,000 shares. The market price may be 179p to 182p, and a call costs 17p for each share. The strike price – the price at your option will let you buy GEC shares – will be 182p. Add 17p to 182p, plus £35 dealing costs, and you are breaking even when GEC top 202½p. For every 1p that GEC rise thereafter, you make a profit of £10. The following calculation may make this clearer

Outgoings Buy 1,000 GEC call options at 17p.	Cost £170
Dealing charges	£35
Exercise option, but 1,000 GEC at 182p.	Cost £1,820
Total buying costs	£2,025

Break-even price for GEC option is 202½p a share (£2,025 divided by 1,000)

Income: Sell 1,000 GEC at 203½p £2,035

So 1p rise in GEC share price equals £10 profit.

At any time during the three month life of the option, you could exercise it, buy 1,000 GEC shares, sell them in the market, and take your profit. Most option players have no intention of using the option to buy the shares and keep them – though sometimes people can add quietly to share stakes that way.

It may be tempting to take up the shares when an option is not going your way. Resist it. Take the loss, and write it off. Do not commit more money to a losing trade.

PUT OPTIONS

Put options are like calls, but geared to a fall in the price. You may think GEC will drop significantly over the next three months. A put option costing 17p will buy the right to sell GEC during those three months at the strike price. The strike price will be 179p. The total cost of 1,000 put options will be £204, including dealing charges. So you need GEC to fall by just under 20½p before you break even. For every 1p fall thereafter, you make £10 profit.

If GEC fall to 145p middle price, and you are able to buy 1,000 shares at 146p, you will be able to exercise your right to sell those 1,000 shares at 179p. That is a profit of 33p a share. Multiply 33p by 1,000, and you have £330. Deduct the option cost of £204, leaving a profit of £126.

The whole exercise is like buying a share, and selling it later at a profit. All you have done is reversed the order, buying at a low price, and selling at the higher price fixed in advance with the option.

In the GEC put example, only £204 was at risk, and it yielded a profit of £126, a high percentage return inside three months. In reality, GEC is usually too stolid a share to allow such fun. What you really need is a more volatile stock, one which moves sharply up or down.

DOUBLE OPTIONS

Double options are expensive. They give the right to buy or sell at the strike price over a three month period. Most punters will not bother.

PROTECTING PROFITS WITH OPTIONS

Options are not just for gambling. They can be used to guard against losses. If you fear the market may tumble, but cannot bear to part with some old favourite, you can have your cake and eat it – at a price. Sell the shares, and buy a call option in them. That way you unlock your capital, and can pop it somewhere safe to sit out the storm. Get it wrong, and you can use your option to buy back into your favourite at the strike price, even if it has gone racing ahead. If the market does tumble, and your share with it, all you have lost is your option money – and that is covered partly by the interest you have been earning on the capital you took out.

Stand the exercise on its head, and you can use options to protect a profit, too. If you fear a flop-out, keep the shares and buy a put. If the fall comes, you will make money on the put to compensate for what you have lost on the shares. This only makes sense, of course, if your shares recover, Otherwise you would have been better with a straightforward sale.

These option protection policies are for the faint-hearted investor. Anyone who paid attention in the earlier part of the book will have little truck with them. Far better to cut losses quickly, and hope to buy back more cheaply later. Have the courage of your convictions.

TAKING OPTION MONEY

Similar considerations apply, less forcefully, to taking option money. If this sounds too confusing, skip it. Never get into anything you do not understand. But for every option someone buys, someone is selling.

If you buy a call, someone takes the call money you spend in return for agreeing for three months to sell shares if you should exercise that call. Because there is a market-maker in the middle, taking his turn, the taker of option money does not get the full amount the buyer is paying. So while it might cost 17p to buy a call in GEC, someone taking that call money might get only 12p. If the call is not exercised, you do not sell your GEC shares, and get 12p for what turns out to be nothing. The snag is that, if GEC soars, the stock will be taken away. You are effectively forced to sell at the 182p strike price, plus 12p, when the shares have soared over 200p.

All sorts of plays can be constructed around taking option money. It may be possible to take call, put or double option money at the same time, and so on.

Conventional options can be used in clever combinations, but require careful understanding and a quick eye for an opportunity. If you want to try it, be sure your boker knows what he is doing. Be guided by your broker.

PLAYING THE MARKET WITH A BOOKIE

It is possible to gamble in the share market through IG Index, the City's own bookmaker. IG Index takes bets on market moves, and dealing costs can be less than stock market commissions. Profits are free of tax. Watch out, though. Many of the bets can have quite a downside if they go wrong. Check the rules carefully.

TAX

Tax. Do not worry about it. Concentrate on making the gains. The first £5,800 of realised gains is exempt from tax in 1992-93. The figure is changed each year. You pay tax at your top rate on gains over that level.

Before you count the profits, you can knock off any losses realised in that tax year. Then you apply an indexation allowance, meant to offset the impact of inflation on shares you have held for a while. It is a complicated formula. working by reference to a table of allowances. Your tax inspector will help you sort it out.

Both husband and wife are eligible for the gains allowance, so it makes sense for married couples to split their portfolio between them. You can also invest through a tax free Personal Equity Plan. So there is ample room for most average investors to shelter from tax. It is worth taking some profits towards the year-end to make the most of your exemption limit, if it suits you. Do not let tax planning dictate your investment decisions.

BED AND BREAKFAST

If you are doing well, it might make sense to 'bed and breakfast' some profits, or establish some losses. Your broker will tell you how to do it. Basically, it involves selling shares one night, and buying back the next day in order to establish a gain or a loss. If you have not used all of your exempt allowance in one year, it might be as well to crystallise a profit to use it up. It also establishes a new base price from which to calculate future capital gains.

PERKS

Everyone loves something for nothing. No matter how trivial the gifts, shareholders flock to annual meetings where something is given away. And they love shares which provide special privileges – perks – to investors.

They range from cheap trips on Cunard liners to handsome reductions on houses from Barratt Developments or Bellway, and take in cheap cars, meals, books and much else.

The list changes all of the time. Some companies require investors to own 1,000 shares, some have no minimum. The best way of finding out what is on offer is to write to stockbrokers Seymour Pierce Butterfield at 24, Chiswell Street, London, EC1Y 4TY for their book on concessionary discounts. This lists the lot, conditions and all. It costs £5, but the brokers offer a £5 voucher which can be set off against commission charges if you should go on to buy shares through them.

Obviously no-one who has waded through this book would be so foolish as to buy shares in a dud company just to get the perks. Would they?

CHAPTER FOURTEEN
TRADED OPTIONS

Stock Exchange officials and brokers will tell you the Traded Options Market offers an invaluable means of controlling and reducing risk – a sensible way for the sophisticated investor to protect himself, and perhaps make more money. Quite so. What they might forget to mention is that this is the hottest spot on the share casino, where you can double or treble your stake in hours. If you are very lucky – or have inside information – you might multiply it tenfold. And the most you can lose, unless you play an especially risky way, is your original stake money.

Corporate raiders use it to build quiet stakes in target companies, hitting traded options before they begin buying the shares. No matter how they may deny it, insider action also happens in traded options. And big investment houses use it to help manipulate prices in the real stock market.

It allows individuals to punt relatively small amounts of cash and control much larger chunks of shares. Get it right, and you can – literally – buy for 1p, and sell for 10p within weeks, maybe less. Winning odds of ten to one are not that common – but they do happen. The chances of doubling your money are very much better.

Make no mistake, though. The risks of losing are high. The old warning has to be hammered home. Do not play traded options with money you cannot afford to lose. YOU WILL LOSE. Start with a limited amount of fun money. If you can afford it, set aside £1,000, and be prepared to kiss it goodbye. Look upon it as the cost of learning – and even then, learning only your first few lessons. Perhaps you will be lucky. Perhaps you will not lose your first £1,000. Maybe the odds will be kind.

In 1989, one player using a broker in Manchester took a few thousand pounds, and made £3m in traded options very quickly. The last I heard, he had dropped a good chunk of it, and gambled £900,000 on the FTSE Index traded options. A few weeks later, he must have been over £1m ahead again.

Terrific. But how many of us would play that way? Our punter must have had nerves of steel, or a skull of solid concrete. The temptation to cash in and sit on the winnings long before

£1m would have been irresistible to most people. It seems foolish not to suggest that anyone who gets, say, £100,000 ahead should not take most of their profits, tuck them away, and sit on their hands for at least three months. That way, you might regain some sensible perspective on the value of money, instead of getting caught up in romantic nonsense about riding a winning streak.

Our anonymous gambler, though, represents the glorious dream. If you are very good, or very lucky, you can make a quick fortune in traded options. I cannot make a serious attempt to analyse the sophisticated strategies which some investment houses use. They are backed by computer power and experts who devote every waking minute to exploiting small anomalies between option rates and share prices.

Expensive and extremely complicated books will give you some guidance on that. It is not for us. As a starter, I can only try to show how relatively simple strategies can be used to make high returns, and how the most unsophisticated play can yield big profits, if you pick the right stock at the right time. In the end, that matters most – picking the right share.

As ever, do not allow yourself to be intimidated by the idea that traded options are too complicated. They can be used as simple gambling counters by anyone prepared to devote time and thought to mastering how they work. Move at your own pace. Never try anything which baffles you, just because someone else says it is good (though you will probably only really begin to get to grips with traded options by actually doing a deal or two). Never be put off by suggestions that this is a market for the big boys alone.

It is not. Traded options can be as simple or as complicated as you want to make them. The small investor can use them to make big profits – with shrewd trading, or with sheer good luck. But they do involve FAST-MOVING, QUICK-STRIKING, HIGH RISK.

WHAT ARE TRADED OPTIONS?

Traded options are broadly similar to the conventional options covered earlier. A call gives the right to buy certain shares at a fixed price during the life of that option. A put option gives the right to sell the shares at a fixed price during the life of that option. The buyer of the option does not have to exercise it. At its daftest, the buyer can walk away, forget about it, write it off. The buyer has absolutely no cash commitment beyond the cost of the option (and, of course, the dealing expenses, which amount to standard stockbroking levels).

Where traded options differ from conventional options is that the options themselves can be bought and sold – traded – during their life. Traded options, then, are like mini-shares, with a value of their own.

This is potentially an enormous advantage. At any time in the life of a traded option, you can sell it. So even if you buy a traded option which does not work out, there is the chance of selling it to avoid a total loss – provided you act before it falls too far, or gets too close to the end of its life.

HOW LONG TRADED OPTIONS LAST

Wonderful. And this need be no desperate, break-neck sprint. Traded options have a decent life, enough to allow you to take a considered view of what to do if the price starts moving against you.

Traded options are created with a clearly defined life span, with regular expiry dates. These are fixed at three-monthly intervals, so each option runs for either three months, six months, or nine months. When one three month cycle ends, a new option is introduced, expiring nine months out.

For example, Superstock International may start with options which expire in April, July, and October. At a pre-determined date in April, all of the Superstock April traded options will expire. A new series will be introduced, with an expiry date in January of the following year – nine months hence. When you deal, it is important to check the actual expiry date. Your broker should be able to give you a calendar. They are normally in the second half of the relevant month.

WHAT THE PRICES MEAN

Look at any display of traded option prices, and there is more than one set of prices for each expiry date. For each call (buy) and put (sell) option, there will options with at least two fixed expiry – or exercise – prices (often more) at each of the three expiry dates. When they start life, these options will be set at prices either side of the then current market price of the underlying share. So if Superstock shares are trading at 130p, there will be traded options at 120p and 140p, one with a life of three months, another expiring in six months' time, and another after nine months.

That way, you will have a simple table when a new options share is introduced. Superstock will have traded options – both puts and calls – looking like this –

April	July	October
120p	120p	120p
140p	140p	140p

If Superstock shares leap above 140p, and stay there for a certain number of days, the Traded Options Market will create a new series of options expiring at 160p. If the price falls below 120p, a new series will be brought in at 110p. It is a routine facility to keep the market working.

It means that after a spell of up and down activity in Superstock, the original traded options table could look like this

April	July	October
110p	110p	110p
120p	120p	120p
140p	140p	140p
160p	160p	160p

While the exercise prices rise by 10p in the lower brackets, they go up by 20p above 140p. That, again, is routine. The higher a price, the less the proportional impact of a 10p change. Correspondingly, when the share price gets above 300p, option exercise prices are set 30p apart.

EXERCISE PRICES

The lists above simply cover what are called the exercise prices. If you decide to use your right to buy or sell the actual shares, you are exercising the option. The price you buy or sell the shares at is the exercise price. So, in the table above, there are options which allow you to buy (call) or sell (put) shares in Superstock at either 110p, 120p, 140p, or 160p – at the expiry date either in April, July, or October.

PREMIUMS

Exercise prices are not the ones which matter most. They are only a label. They simply describe the option you are buying. So the Superstock July 120p call gives you the right to buy shares in Superstock at 120p in July. And the Superstock October 140p put gives you the right to sell Superstock shares at 140p in October.

What really counts is what you pay when you buy the options, or what you get when you sell. That is called the premium, and determines whether you make a profit or a loss.

In most newspapers which carry traded option prices, the premium is listed in the sections to the right, under the 'Calls' heading, or under the 'Puts' heading. Those 'Calls' and 'Puts' sections themselves are divided into three for the three-month, six-month, or nine-month expiry dates. A typical newspaper display of traded options in Superstock, with the current share price in brackets beneath the company name, might look as follows -

OPTION	Exercise price	CALLS			PUTS		
		Apr	Jul	Oct	Apr	Jul	Oct
Superstock (128p)	110p	24p	29p	36p	1p	3p	5p
	120p	13p	17p	20p	5p	9p	12p
	140p	6p	8p	10p	18p	23p	27p
	160p	1p	2p	3p	36p	40p	44p

Looking at the 'Calls', this shows that if you want the right to buy shares in Superstock for 110p in April, it will cost 24p a share. You are effectively betting that Superstock shares will rise from their current 128p to more than 134p (the 110p exercise price, plus the 24p premium) before your option expires in April.

If you buy Superstock October 140p calls, it will cost 10p. You are betting that, before your option expires nearly nine months away in October, Superstock shares will rise to more than 150p (the 140p exercise price, plus the 10p premium). And so on.

Scanning the 'Puts', for 9p you can buy an option to sell Superstock at 120p in July. You would be betting that the Superstock price will fall below 111p (the 120p exercise price, minus the 9p premium) before the option runs out in July.

Or if you buy the October 160p puts for 44p, you will be gambling on the price falling below 116p (160p exercise price, minus 44p) before October.

CONTRACTS – THE TRADING UNIT

There is a minimum size for each deal. That is called a contract, and each contract normally represents an option on 1,000 shares. This varies now and then, but usually only for shares with a price over £10. Then each contract normally involves 100 shares.

As a result, each 1p of option premium normally translates into a cost of £10 for each contract (1,000 multiplied by 1p equals £10). So our Superstock April 110p calls at 24p premium will cost £240 for each contract, the October 140p calls at 10p will cost £100 a contract, the July 120p puts at 9p will cost £90 for one contract, and the October 160p puts at 44p will cost £440 for each contract.

The same multiple comes through to your profits and losses. For every contract, each 1p change in the premium means you have made or lost £10.

A SIMPLE PROFIT PLAY

Study the table. Think about it. Once you know what the figures mean, it is fairly simple. At its most basic, that tells you all you need to know. If you think a particular share is going to rise or fall , and if there are traded options in it (quite a big 'if' that, though additional shares are being brought into the net all of the time), you can control a far larger number of those shares by using traded options than by buying the shares. If you are betting on a rise, buy a call. To bet on a fall, buy a put. Go back to our Superstock price table. If you expect a big rise in the next six months, and you have £600 to gamble, you can buy about 468 shares at 128p each. Or you can buy three July 120p call contracts for £170 a time (the premium is 17p, but each contract is for 1,000 shares, so each contract costs £170) to control 3,000 shares, with £90 left over. Because you have three contracts, each 1p price change means you gain or lose £30.

Say you get it just about right, and Superstock shares touch 140p. By buying the shares, you will have made a profit of just over £56 (multiply 468 by 12p equals £56.16p). By buying the options, you will have made £90 (the 120p call options should have risen from 17p to at least 20p to match the 140p market price, a rise of 3p. Each 1p change is worth £10 a contract. Three contracts are worth £30 for each 1p change. Multiply £30 by three equals £90). And you still have the £90 you did not invest.

The arithmetic looks better the higher your shares rise. Say Superstock went to 145p. Then the shares would show a profit of just under £90. Your traded options would be £240 ahead (Profit of 8p on each contract. Multiply £30 by eight equals £240). Plus £90 not invested.

And if Superstock touched 150p, the options look still further ahead. The gain on buying the shares would have been nearly £103. But the traded option profit would have been £390 (Profit of 13p on option, so multiply £30 by 13 equals £390), plus £90 not invested.

Terrific? Perhaps. We have ignored the cost of buying and selling. That would have cut profits sharply, especially at the lower level of gains. More important, the traded option player has taken a vastly greater risk than the share buyer. If the Superstock price had not moved over the six months, the share buyer would still have had shares worth just under £600. The option player would have lost every penny, except the £90 he did not spend.

If Superstock shares had fallen to, say, 110p, the share buyer would have an investment worth £514, a loss of around £86. Again, the traded option punter would have lost every penny, and be nursing only the £90 left over. Thankfully the fall in the share price would not have brought any extra liability. That is a crucial advantage of traded options – if you stick to buying calls or puts, you cannot lose more than your stake money.

Make no mistake, it is easy to lose that stake money. The figures above look persuasive. But many small traded option punters do get wiped out quickly – though the fun lasts longer than the 3.30 at Epsom. Or last Saturday's treble chance coupon.

Buy a traded call in a bid target (as one major broking house did in large numbers on the day before the abortive Kingfisher bid for Dixons), and you can clean up when the bid comes.

No complication. The shares rise, and the options with them. Usually options gains are in massively greater proportions than profits on the shares. The lucky, or well-informed, sell the options and waltz off with an enormous haul. Easy.

Normally it is not as simple as that. Option prices do not go up in a straight line, linked to the underlying share price. Sometimes the shares rise, and the call options fall. Usually this is a result of the interaction between the two main elements which determine the level of an option price – the intrinsic value, and the time value. Sometimes there is an element of market manipulation, of course.

INTRINSIC VALUE

Go back to our Superstock options. The premium on the Superstock April 110p call is 24p, while the share price is 128p. In theory, you could exercise the option, take the shares for 110p, and sell them for 128p, a gain of 18p. That 18p is known as the intrinsic value – the locked-in gain, if you like. Since the option costs 24p, of course, that 18p is not profit. It covers much of the premium you are paying.

IN THE MONEY

An option which has an intrinsic value – or an exercise price below the market price of the underlying share – is said to be 'In-the-Money'.

OUT OF THE MONEY

By contrast, look at the Superstock April 140p call, with a premium of 6p. The exercise price is above the underlying share price of 128p. There is no immediate built-in gain. Such an option is 'Out-of-the-Money'. Logically enough, if the option exercise price is the same as the underlying share price, the option is 'At-the-Money'. So if Superstock shares were 140p in the market, the April 140p calls would be 'At-the-Money'.

TIME VALUE

Option premiums are not just determined, however, by the price of the underlying shares. They are also determined by how long the option has to run – the time value. Clearly time has a very real value for option traders, and the more time there is before the option expires, the greater the value.

Go back again to our first example, Superstock April 110p calls, with a premium of 24p. With Superstock shares at 128p, the option is 'In-the-Money', and has an intrinsic value of 18p. The other 6p of the premium is accounted for by time value – what you pay for the chance that the shares will rise above 128p (and effectively above 134p) before the option expires in April.

Time value does not run out evenly over the life of the option. Experts use a fancy formula to determine it, but all you need to know is that the value declines at an accelerating rate as it approaches the end of life. So you need to keep it very much in mind, especially when you get within 30 days of the end.

VOLATILITY

Option prices are also partly determined by volatility, the violence and frequency with which share prices move. Looking at conventional options, I suggested that GEC was an unexciting example, because the shares were pretty stolid. They do not move sharply, and over recent years, have traded in a fairly narrow range.

What you want, above all, is price action. You can get a good clue to the chances by studying past price movements – no guarantees, of course. When something exceptional has taken place – a bid, or news of a profit slump – you clearly must take it into account in measuring activity. Option experts have systems for measuring volatility, and helping determine whether particular option rates are good or bad value. Obviously an option in a stock which normally bobs busily about holds more promise of reward than a sluggard, and so the option rate may be a higher. Keep it in mind, and ask your broker to check volatility before buying.

THE MATHEMATICS

Assessing volatility brings us to the brink of the more sophisticated stuff. Professional option traders run a variety of factors into their judgement of option values. They use complex mathematical formulae. Best-known is the Black-Scholes model. I do not understand it. Many of the users do not. If you want to know, most options brokers will give you a quick view of how Black-Scholes rates your prospective punt. You do not have to know what it means – but listen to what they say if they tell you if it is working against you. Do not ignore the advice. It means that the professionals will be guided by it, and will tend to shy clear of your option if it looks too expensive. You could be right – if there is a bid, or your underlying reason for buying is spot on – but you would be paying over the odds for your bet, your traded option.

DIVIDENDS

Dividend payments also complicate the issue. The notion is that option prices take account of dividends well ahead of their payment date. Share prices fall when they go ex-dividend – when the buyer of the shares is no longer entitled to collect the latest dividend cheque. It forms a pre-arranged and well understood fall in the share price. It will drive call option prices down, and raise the value of put options.

Because everyone knows about it in advance, it may not have any great impact. It should have been taken into account in setting the price. And a dividend of 1p on a share selling at 250p will not matter much in any case. But the market does not always have it fully covered. A 5p dividend on a 100p share could make a big difference to a call option near the end of its life. So keep an eye out for dividends.

WRITING OPTIONS

Our examples of how call and put options work have demonstrated the chance of making money by straightforward option purchases when you think a share is going to rise or fall. But there is another important aspect to the options game – writing them. An options writer simply sells the put or call which someone else buys. Go back to our Superstock table. If you write an April 120p call, you earn a 13p premium. If you write a 140p July put, you take a 23p premium. And so on.

WRITING COVERED CALLS

What you are doing is effectively betting that, as above, Superstock will not go above 133p before the April expiry date, or fall below 117p before the July date. If you hold the shares, writing a call is a handy way of generating extra income, so long as they do not move out of line, and the option is exercised against you, forcing you to give up the stock. Money for almost nothing. As an option writer, what you really want is a share that goes nowhere much while the option is open – the opposite to the volatile stock you wanted when buying a put or call.

Writing an option also acts as a possible way of selling above the current price. Writing that April 120p call for a 13p premium means you are ready to sell at 133p, when the market price is 128p. If you are prepared to take a longer view, using our table, you could have sold (or written) an October 120p call for 20p, effectively getting out at 140p. The careful investor, of course, would be sure to hold the shares until October, just in case they did have to be delivered. If the option is not exercised, you will still have the shares, plus your 20p premium.

If you are nervous about the market, it is a way of generating extra protection. Again using the 13p premium on an April 120p, you can see the price fall from the market level of 128p to 115p before it has taken a toll on your investment.

NAKED WRITING

You can play the same game without holding the shares. It is risky – very risky – and can lead to unquantified losses. When you sell a call, or write one, you are called a naked writer if you do not hold the underlying stock. If it works, and the option simply lapses, it could mean you get the premium for nothing. If the shares do not rise all of the way to cover the full premium, you can still buy the stock and cover yourself without disaster.

But what if the unexpected should happen? What if Superstock gets a bid at 250p early in April. The share price will rise to 250p, perhaps 260p if there is speculation on a counter-bid.

The April 120p call could rocket to 135p, maybe more. The option could be exercised against you, and you have to deliver stock you have not got. You would have to go into the market and pay 260p. Since all that you have received is the 13p premium, you will have to find an extra 247p a share. Oh dear. DO NOT DO IT.

Sensibly, the market rules try to guard against reckless naked writing. Those who write options are required to pledge collateral to the value of a margin requirement. This is related to the underlying share price, and the option exercise price being calculated as 20pc of the value of the underlying contract size, plus or minus the amount the option is in or out of the money. Complicated? Sure. Your broker will tell you. But if just thinking about it puts you off, great.

WRITING PUTS

The same sort of reasoning applies to writing puts. Effectively, there is no such thing as a covered put writer. In theory, whether you hold the shares or not, you could have a block of shares put on you, forcing you to buy. That will happen when the shares have gone down, so you will end up with an extra lot of duds – not what you intended. Because you have taken a premium when you sold, or wrote, the put, that will reduce your purchase price. Anyone who writes put options must be happy to buy the stock at below the current level. You have to be able to lay your hands on the cash. Will you really want to be landed with a lot of the shares when the price is tumbling? Maybe not. So be careful.

What really happens, in most cases, is that the put writer has to buy the put option back in the market, effectively neutralising his liability. That can be expensive, with the put price rising as the share price tumbles. So beware.

STRADDLES, SPREADS AND SO ON

There are all sorts of strategies which can be devised by a using a combination of options. A straddle involves buying a put and a call with the same exercise price and expiry date. Or you can use a straddle, exploiting relative discrepancies between option prices within the same class. The opportunities are endless, and require careful, detailed understanding. Do not try them until you really know what you are doing. Leading brokers have handy guides, which they may send you. The Stock Exchange itself has published a booklet called 'Strategies' which gives an excellent outline of the most common plays.

It is common to hear punters complaining about the way the market operates. Market-makers are accused of running very wide spreads between buy and sell prices, and of failing to move rates properly in response to underlying share price changes. What would you expect? Real life on the option market is not simple. Everyone is out to make a profit. Do not imagine things will run just as you expect them.

Above all, remember the basics. No matter how clever the option trade may seem, and how cheap the rate looks, you have to get the share direction right first. Do not lose sight of trading in the underlying company. In the end, that is the most important influence. And then? CUT LOSSES QUICKLY, AND RUN YOUR PROFITS. Because there is a limited life to options, it is hard to operate a stop-loss system. But do not be silly and let your emotions rule your head. You will come unstuck far faster as a fool in the options market than you will by playing shares alone.

PLAYING FOOTSIE

There is one special facility in the options market which is unrivalled by the share game. You can take a view on the overall direction of share prices by playing Footsie, the FT-SE 100 Share Index.

There are Footsie options contracts which operate in much the same fashion as options on individual shares. You can buy options on the index running several months ahead. You are betting on which way the index will move. Obviously you do not get a basket of shares if you exercise the option, simply the cash difference between your price and the FTSE level.

Playing Footsie can be useful when you are worried about a possible market slump. Or if you think there may be a rise, but are not quite ready to plunge in yet. Above all, it can be a great insurance policy, allowing you either to sit with your shares and cover a general market move, or to sell your portfolio, bank the cash, and keep an interest in the market at low cost through a Footsie option. Talk to your broker.

CHAPTER FIFTEEN
NAMES TO WATCH

Nothing lasts for ever in the share game. But certain names seem to come up, time and again, chaps always ready to try to build businesses or improve share prices by doing deals. Patterns of behaviour rarely change decisively. One a deal-doer, always a deal-doer, it seems. After a while, you may learn to recognise them. Some names are always worth backing, some get it right some of the time, others . . . well, judge for yourself.

Keeping track of who's who is hard, especially for those outside the City. Hence the following modest list of the names to watch, good, bad and indifferent, a few of the would-be movers and shakers, with my own personal verdict on how I would view their progress.

Actually naming names introduces a practical element absent from most investment books, but it does have drawbacks. Some of my opinions might keep you out of winners, and encourage you to back a loser or two. No-one gets it right every time. And obviously such a list cannot be bang up to date. Dealers move so quickly, and the ones you may want to know about most may be the ones who have not been round long enough to get on any list. But every little helps. Past performance is not necessarily a guide to the future, and the luck of anyone on the list could change.

For good measure, I have thrown in a few of the names from the share-pushing scene in the eighties. If you are approached by companies associated with them, put down the phone.

So here it goes, my personal register of names to watch, with my own subjective opinion of how to view their chances. As always, unless you are very sure of what you are doing, err on the side of caution.

AITKEN, Tim. Built Aitken Hume well initially, then rescued TV-am. Recently active on US company scene. Controversial but energetic approach. Worth backing.

AITKEN, Ronnie. Veteran company doctor. Has his City critics, tread cautiously.

ASHCROFT, Michael. Chairman and chief executive of car auctions and security group ADT, sometime dealer in share stakes. Highly controversial style. Too widely criticised in the City to back. Stay clear.

ASPINALL, Damian. Son of John Aspinall, casino operator and friend of Sir James Goldsmith. Modest success in property in the eighties, popped up at Caverdale in 1991 with heavyweight shareholder support from dad's pals. Interesting, but watch carefully.

BAILEY, Denis. Stockbroker at Hichens Harrison, involved in promotion of many smallish companies. Uneven record. Treat with care.

BENTLEY, John. Successful seventies operator, struggling to sustain public company success in eighties. Problems in nineties with A. Brown suggest caution.

BERRY, Tony. Built Blue Arrow with massive fan club until share placing controversy and market collapse. Moved into Business Technology Group, initially disappointing. Survived turmoil on Tottenham Hotspur board. Tread carefully.

BIERMANN, Hugo. Some success with Thomson T-Line before sale to Ladbroke. Moved in at Pathfinder in first stage of building early in 1992. Worth watching.

BLOOMFIELD, Paul. Property man associated with Clegg in building Mountleigh, though attracted criticism as he was undischarged bankrupt (now discharged) for much of that time. Expert but controversial dealer. Could generate interest, but tread cautiously.

BOWKETT, Alan. Great success in private company encouraged big investors to install him with lavish options at Berisford International early in 1992. Great promise.

BUCKLEY, Michael. Racehorse owner. Indifferent share performance while he has been at several small companies including Wilton Group. Treat cautiously.

BURNE, David. Former financial journalist. Linked with small companies in eighties, unable to sustain success. Approach with caution.

CLEGG, Tony. Built Mountleigh into highly successful property group in early eighties only to see it run into problems as he hit health trouble and sold out. Could have useful following, but take care.

COWAN, Peter. Director of successful Prestwich Holdings under Paul Levinson in eighties, started to build useful healthcare products distribution business at Intercare. Worth watching.

CRAMER, Guy. Associate of Peter Clowes, cleared at Barlow Clowes trial. Stay clear.

d'ABO, Jennifer. Well-fancied company director, revived Ryman, disappointed at Stormgard. Worth watching, with care.

DANE, Dan. Insurance man, involved in Renaissance, a US share heavily pushed by defunct dealing firm Tudorbury. Keep clear.

de SAVARY, Peter. Gossip column favourite, with high publicity private enterprises. Brief disappointing public company exposure. View public company moves with caution.

DONOUGHUE, Lord. Former stockbroker. Maxwell associate.

DUGGAN, John. Property man, briefly at head of Mountleigh, then at Cabra caught in wrangle over Fulham and Chelsea football grounds. Think twice.

EARL, Peter. Energetic merchant banking maverick, built Tranwood Earl business, associated with possible remarkable reverse bid for Storehouse. Enterprising ideas, erratic achievement. Think twice.

ELLINGHAM, David. Did brilliantly with Peter James in building WSL, disappointed at Business Technology, but has useful knack of making money. Worth watching.

FERGUSON LACEY, Graham. Born-again Christian. Terrific run in early eighties, then hit problems with company collapses. Resurfaced in UK from US in 1991 at Aviva and other companies to widespread adverse comment. Stay clear.

FETTERMAN, Norman. Built Barham Group and made marvellous sale of it to IBC just before 1987 crash. Then into Oakwood which went into receivership late 1989. Popped up at rag trader Helene early 1992. Well-regarded, but may find it hard to repeat early success.

FITCH, Billy. Associate of Graham Ferguson Lacey.

FORSYTH, Stephen. With brother Jamie built shell company Doloswella and made brief impact in eighties at Leisure Investments, buying companies from Peter de Savary before collapse. Stay clear.

GOMMES, John. Controversial company director in seventies, then prominent in tip sheet trade, did well at Chartsearch. Enterprising. Worth backing.

GORDON, Murray. Retail veteran, sold Combined English Stores brilliantly to Next in eighties. Useful following.

GREYSTOKE, Andrew. Director of several small companies in eighties and early nineties. Attracted considerable controversy, disappointing share performance. Avoid.

HAMILTON, RAI. Successful insurance salesman, main mover behind Tudorbury Securities, later Alexander Securities, eighties telephone share selling operations. Stay clear.

HARGRAVE, Stephen. Former financial journalist. Did well rebuilding Pathfinder Group, small-scale. Youngish. Promising.

HINCHLIFFE, Stephen. Left James Wilkes early in 1992 in middle of bid from Petrocon. Also left Lynx. Controversial background. Tread cautiously.

HOARE, Charles. Merchant banker in seventies, later chairman of Geers Gross advertising agents, and associated with Robert Fraser investment banking business. On board of share selling firm Alexander Securities ahead of collapse. Stay clear.

HODGSON, Howard. Built up substantial funeral business from base of Hodgson Holdings. Sold out and now offers franchise ideas and such. Worth following if he returns to public company.

HUTCHINGS, Greg. One of the great successes of eighties, ex-Hanson man built F.H. Tomkins brilliantly, then took smaller interest in Mosaic. First class.

JAMES, David. High profile, much-fancied company doctor, hit headlines in Eagle Trust rescue, re-shaped Davies & Newman. Great and good.

JAMES, Peter. Brilliant highly profitable transformation and sale of original shell WSL. Then at Business Technology Group where shares peaked over 200p and fell sharply, linked to Tony Berry. Tread cautiously.

JAY, Peter. Former TV-am director, Maxwell associate.

JESSEL, Oliver. Sixties and seventies company man. Main company collapsed in seventies, surfaces sometimes in small situations. Think twice.

JOHNSON, Luke. Former stockbroking analyst. Recovered to save and rebuild shell company P.E. Kemp. Also director of Automobiles of Distinction with Richard Palmer into promising European Motor. Worth watching.

KENT, Andrew. Formerly associated with stockbroker T.C. Coombs which was linked to several small, speculative Australian companies, and small, speculative UK companies. Avoid.

KENT, Peter. Ran Lancashire and Yorkshire Investment, investment advice firm which closed in early nineties after FIMBRA investigation and *Daily Mail* criticism. Avoid.

LEVINSON, Paul. Started cut-price video revolution launching the Video Collection at Prestwich Holdings in eighties. Sold well. Worth following if he returns to public scene.

LING, Philip. Former assistant to Oliver Jessel, attempted ambitious engineering reorganisation at Haden MacLellan, hampered by 1987 stock market crash. Worth watching.

LUCAS, Michael. Chairman of BOM Holdings, criticised in DTI investigation into company's affairs. Former shareholder in share pushers Tudorbury. Avoid.

MARWAN, Dr Ashraf. Influential Egyptian businessman, once involved with Lonrho, and linked to small merchant bank Tranwood Earl. Successfully traded stake in Fleet Holdings, more recently building stake in Cabra Estates. Think twice.

McGOWAN, Brian. Joined Nigel Rudd to make Williams Holdings one of the most successful eighties conglomerates. Worth following.

MACGREGOR, Sir Ian. Elderly US banker, made his name at National Coal Board. Spoilt his reputation through his post as long-serving director of controversial property group Mountleigh. Takes on troubled companies. Tread cautiously.

MATTOCK, Clive. Stockbroker, formerly with Fiske & Co, now Ellis and Partners. Former director of investment group UTC which hit problems in late eighties. Controversial style. Linked to several shell situations. Worth watching, but take care.

MILLER, Neil. Not a deal-doer, but definitely a man to avoid. Former stock salesman at Harvard Securities, he worked for RAI Hamilton at Tudorbury, and led the team and London & Norwich which sold shares in a totally dud company called Silverton.

MILLS, Christopher. Revamped several small companies using US oil tax losses, linked with Lord Stevens and Invesco MIM. Director of Danka Business Systems in nineties. Worth following.

MORRIS, Stephen. Behind Orbital Communications public share float abandoned after *Daily Mail* criticism in late eighties. Stay clear.

MORTON, Bob. Successful stakebuilder in smallish companies. Vistec and Albrighton in nineties. Good fan club. Promising.

MUNRO-WILSON, Brod. Scored great success with hand in flotation of Body Shop. Launched several small companies through Munro Corporate, with several failures. Stay clear.

NOONAN, Robert. Property man, involved in Marler Estates. Tread cautiously.

NURSE, Christopher. Former merchant banker, moved in at industrial ceramics group Hewitt in 1991. Promising.

OPPENHEIM, Nick. Successful in eighties in smallish situations. Floated Whitegate Leisure, hit problems in nineties. Stay clear.

PALMER, Richard. Did well with Western Motor in eighties, disappointed with Automobiles of Distinction. May do better now into European Motor. Promising.

QUAYLE, David. One of the founders of B & Q diy business. Since director of several companies, including chairman of video rental group Cityvision at one stage. Worth backing.

ROBERTSON, Sir Lewis. Veteran company doctor. Solid reputation.

ROWLAND, David 'Spotty'. Won reputation in seventies as youthful head of Fordham property group. Less successful with Williams Hudson, which hit problems, and more recently, Inoco. Stay clear.

RUDD, Graham. Brother of highly successful Nigel at Williams Holdings. Did brilliantly initially at Thomas Robinson, left in nineties after profits collapse. Might run again, but tread cautiously.

RUDD, Nigel. Half of pair with Brian McGowan which built Williams Holdings brilliantly. Less successful with housebuilder Raine Industries. Worth following.

SEDGHI, Bijan. Trying to build Bromsgrove Industries, stuck with it well through slump. Worth watching.

SHUTE, Roger. Well-fancied boss of BM Group. Worth backing.

SIMONS, Ed. Director of Brent Walker in early days, partner of show-biz ace Harvey Goldsmith in eighties. Initial forays into public company disappointing, but worth watching.

SLATER, Jim. Investment and company guru of sixties and seventies. Minus-millionaire when Slater Walker collapsed in mid-seventies. Still potential following. More likely to be investor than player. Worth watching.

SOLOMON, Sir Harry. Fared brilliantly helping build Hillsdown Holdings, but less successful in nineties. Backed stakes in several smaller companies with uneven results. Watch with care.

STERLING, Freddie. Ran Gresham House investment trust successfully until it hit trouble with unquoted investments. Think twice.

STEVENS, Lord. Chairman of United Newspapers, built his fortune in fund management with Drayton companies and Invesco MIM. Did several deals with his friend Robert Maxwell attracting City criticism. Tread cautiously.

SUGAR, Alan. Made fortune building Amstrad electronics group, moved into Tottenham Hotspur to reshape it. Shrewd dealer. Worth following, but sell when he does.

TAGLIGHT, David. Back-room boy, careful analyst, pops up in smallish situations supporting good company men. Some success in eighties with LDH, rumoured looking at situations in nineties. Worth backing.

THAIN, Greg. Problems with small private companies before going into small public company which disappointed. Controversial style. Tread cautiously.

THOMPSON, David. Founder of highly successful food and diversified conglomerate Hillsdown Holdings. Backed several businesses since with mixed results. Watch with care.

THOMPSON, Richard. Son of David Thompson.

VANDYK, Edward. Grim record with small Over-The-Counter companies in eighties, and at Leisure Investments as it collapsed under Forsyth brothers. Retrieved Courtwell and rebuilt into promising Select Industries, and in background elsewhere. Cautiously optimistic.

VAUGHAN-LEE, Mark. Member of group linked with Lord Stevens and Christopher Mills. Several successful small company revivals. Into Danka Business Systems in nineties. Worth backing.

WILLIAMS, David. Joined Usher-Walker in 1991 with ambitions to build it after period with Mosaic Investments. Promising.

WILLIAMS of Elvel (Lord). Merchant banker, Maxwell associate.

WILMOT, Tom. Built Harvard Securities, controversial telephone share selling and issuing house with closed in eighties. Floated several companies, some winners, some losers. Stay clear.

WOOTLIFF, Stanley. Erratic public company career in eighties. Trying to rebuild Caldwell Investments in nineties. Usually does well for early supporters. Worth backing with care.

WRAY, Nigel. Built fortune in seventies and eighties from original tip sheet base. Director of Carlton Communications and property group Burford. Imaginative and intelligent. Worth backing.

CONCLUSION

Thank you for buying this book. I hope it helps you to profit from the coming share boom. I hope it has helped you realise that you can play the stock market, if you want.

The scene is changing all of the time, but though the day-to-day detail may alter, the basics remain the same. It is your money, so do it your way. But only use what you can afford to lose, only do what you understand, watch out for the angle, and cut your losses quickly.

Above all, have fun. Good luck.